AIKIDO

A I K I D O

Traditional Art & Modern Sport

Brian N. Bagot

(Under the supervision of Sensei Paul McGlone)

The Crowood Press

First published in 1990 by
The Crowood Press Ltd
Gipsy Lane
Swindon
Wiltshire
SN2 6DQ

British Library Cataloguing in Publication Data
Bagot, Brian N.
  Aikido: traditional art & modern sport.
  1. Aikido
  I. Title
  796.8154

ISBN 1 85223 426 1

Acknowledgements
This book could not have been written without the help and
encouragement of Paul McGlone and his students from Poole Aikido, to
all of whom I am deeply indebted. My grateful thanks must also be
extended to Bob Forrest-Webb who has written a foreword on behalf of
the British Aikido Association and has also helped me to put together
the final chapter which deals with areas I am less familiar with. Without
his guidance, I would have been hard put to complete the text. I must
also thank Paul Wildish, Peter Williams and Eddie Ferrie who helped
me with certain photographic material. Thanks must also be expressed
to Bruce Klickstein and Tony Sargeant who have both helped me along
the way and also to the members of the Wareham Zen Judo and Aikido
Club who have suffered under my instruction without (too much)
complaint for so long. Finally, I should like to thank all those who have
helped me, wittingly and unwittingly, in the development of my aikido.

Dedication
This book is dedicated to my first Sensei, Dominick McCarthy, without
whom I would have been ignorant of the ways of the martial arts.
Thank you Mac.

Line illustrations by Janet Sparrow

Typeset by Chippendale Type Limited, Otley, West Yorkshire.
Printed in Great Britain by Redwood Press Limited, Melksham, Wiltshire.

Contents

POEM

Many enemies
surround me
in attack.
Thinking of them as one,
I do battle.

Ueshiba Sensei

Foreword by Haydn Foster

INTEREST BEGETS MEMORY
MEMORY BEGETS LEARNING

I was very pleased to be asked to write the foreword to this book, for as one who has benefited from 35 years of training in aikido, I welcome any effort to introduce and encourage more and more people to practise this martial art.

In attracting new students to our training sessions, we must first get their interest before we can hope to teach them. When training students in complex or technical subjects, there is a great risk of their losing interest if they are confronted by jargon or words and expressions they find difficult to understand. It is a very big step for the student to take when he decides to learn the ideas and methods of the Japanese Master who founded aikido, as they are so different from our Western culture and methods of training. The transition must be made to be as gentle as possible to allow the beginner to get acclimatized. Some authors of text books of a technical nature find it difficult to communicate at the level of understanding of the interested beginner. Aikido is a complex subject and as such there is a need for detailed manuals, which may be used in conjunction with practical instruction and training. There are many good books on the market which meet this need. However, I feel that there is still a need for a book that will provide a simple introduction to aikido, to attract and hold the interest of those who are seeking knowledge of the art. The author has been successful in that his book gently leads the beginner through his or her introduction to an art that must appear a little strange to the uninitiated student with its use of Japanese words and ideas. After reading the author's simple description of the training room (dojo) the beginner will be prepared for the new environment encountered with the practice of aikido.

We cannot learn a skill from books alone, to quote an old training adage, 'Tell me, I will forget. Show me, I will understand. Let me do it and I will remember.' Aikido requires continuous training under the guidance of an experienced teacher to confirm the written words and pictures.

The techniques chosen for inclusion in this book are ideal for the beginner. When dealing with the use of the Sword (Bokken) and Staff (Jo) the author has shown the fundamental relationship between the Sword, Staff and Body in a way that should be readily understood by the student. He has wisely avoided delving too deeply into the more intricate aspects of aikido such as *ki* (inner power) or *kokyu* (breath control). I am sure that in the early stages of their training, beginners will soon realise that *aikido* without *ki* or *kokyu* becomes a poor imitation of the true art.

As a beginner, it was impressed upon

me to become 'one with nature'. It took some years to understand fully what was expected of me, but I gradually realised that it could be taken to mean 'be yourself' – be natural according to nature, do not be an artificial or manufactured being'. The author has intimated this awareness in his book.

His appendices are among the best that I have read and he is to be congratu-lated on producing a book that not only provides an introduction to the art but provides a reference for the serious student. I would recommend it to all who wish to reap the rewards which training in the art of aikido brings.

Haydn Foster
Chief Instructor/Principal Coach
Institute of Aikido

Foreword by Bob Forrest-Webb

I am often asked by beginners in aikido, 'What books should I read?' Until now, it has been a difficult question to answer. There *are* books on aikido – several of them – but their authors presume previous knowledge in their readers or, through thoughtlessness, manage to isolate themselves from the problems that can place a seemingly impenetrable wall before a novice. Brian Bagot's *Aikido: Traditional Art and Modern Sport* offers the beginner a ladder upon which he can begin the long, enjoyable climb towards the unattainable perfection we all seek.

Regardless of the style a novice may choose to follow, the basics of aikido are the roots and trunk of the oak tree from which a hundred branches may grow; all are different, and yet contain the same parental elements. Rather than seeking their superficial or cosmetic dissimilarities, it is far more important to recognise the common factors and enjoy the grandeur of the tree as a whole.

The more open-minded the student remains, the broader the scope for learning. If you isolate yourself by assuming your Sensei teaches the only 'right' way you eliminate the possibility of practising your aikido, and making friends in cities and towns throughout the world. When I travel abroad on holiday, or for work, my *gi* and *hakama* are in my luggage. If you are open-minded, you will be welcomed in every dojo regardless of the form of aikido they follow.

Avoid criticisms of other styles. Even at a very senior grade it is easy to be ill-informed. For example, for years Tomiki aikido was thought by many traditional students to be purely sports orientated – which is quite inaccurate. A Tomiki student's competitive life is relatively short – if he or she competes at all! Aikido offers a lifetime of purposeful interest, and styles tend to merge as pupils progress. It may interest the newcomer to know that Sensei Tetsuro Nariyama, 8th Dan, and rated as the leading Tomiki instructor in the world, was not only a pupil of Tomiki Shihan, but also of the traditional master, Hirakuza Kobayashi, with whom he shares a dojo in Osaka. This combination of styles has made Nariyama Sensei's aikido fluid and powerful, and it is the form currently practised by the majority of Tomiki students.

Within the British Aikido Association, we have the modern Tomiki aikido, and O Sensei's traditional form (Kai Shin Kai), and there are regular exchanges of instructors between the Tomiki and Kai Shin Kai divisions of the organisation. We share our knowledge, and benefit by doing so. Aikido is not simply a matter of harmony between two students in the artificial confines of a dojo – to be totally effective, it must become a natural part of the aikidoka's daily life.

You are embarking on an intriguing journey and I am certain that this book will make a good travelling companion.

Bob Forrest-Webb
Chairman, British Aikido Association

Preface

Aikido may be described as one of the most subtle and sophisticated of the martial arts. It is not only an effective self-defence system but also a method of strengthening the mind and body to produce a more integrated person. The word *aikido* means the way (*do*) of harmony (*ai*) of the spirit (*ki*), and the art was originally developed by Master Morihei Ueshiba from movements contained within the arts of sword and spear fighting, ju jutsu, aiki jutsu and other schools of the martial arts.

Aikido differs from other martial arts in that it is related directly to defence against unprovoked attack. There is no aggressive move in aikido. This is also said of karate and judo, although both of these contain moves which may be used for attack as well as for defence. Aikido has no movements which may be used in an attacking situation.

When you begin to read books written about aikido (and I shall refer to some texts for further reading later on), you quickly note that the accent is heavily upon the development of *ki* (inner energy) and the concentration of that energy at your *hara* (centre of gravity), as well as circularity of the flow of your movements. These concepts are very important to the aikidoka (student of aikido) and the art cannot be properly studied without attention to them. When I was a complete beginner I found that the frequent references to these concepts tended to overshadow the more intricate aspects of the technique; it is just as important to understand these, if not more so at that stage. This confusion led to this book being conceived.

All other works that I have so far come across have been written by high-grade masters who either describe techniques far more advanced than are required by the beginner, or only touch upon a few movements and provide a plethora of variations, which will be of more use to you after some years of training. This book provides both an overview of all the aspects of aikido and gives the beginner an insight into the wealth of technique awaiting him or her. Primarily it is a book for those seeking to learn about aikido compiled by a relative beginner.

With this in mind, I have set out to put together a text which details examples of the basic techniques required for the initial grading syllabus within many clubs. You should bear in mind that every instructor will teach in a different manner, usually in the form that suits his or her own body. This means that probably even the most basic of the techniques will be taught differently in each club. That is certainly the case in every club I have visited. I have therefore tried to condense the many variations within each technique down to the common form and present this to you as the basis for starting to learn the movements, so that you can build on this as you progress in your own club.

As this book was being written, I started teaching a small class at my own dojo (practice hall), and these are the techniques which they are currently learning. I have tried to include everything that could be required by you at the early stages of your training, and have deliberately played down those aspects which involve the use of *ki* (inner energy) and *kokyu* (breath control) in favour of technique application. That is not to say that these will not be mentioned in the text where necessary, but they will play only a minor part.

I am aware that by doing this I leave myself open to criticism for not presenting aikido in its totality, as the application of both *kokyu* and *ki* is as much a part of aikido as the physical techniques. My reasoning is that the majority of students will commence training within a recognised club and they will, no doubt, be lectured on the application of *ki* and the correct way to breathe to such an extent that they will soon become confused. This book will be available to help supplement their learning without concentration upon these more esoteric areas.

During the compilation of this text, some of the techniques have undergone revision in the light of the visit to Britain of Morihiro Saito Sensei. Aikido techniques do not remain static, but tend to develop with time and experience, and the student who begins his learning today will see the techniques change as he progresses slowly along the way. Changes come from the instructors as they gain experience and alter their methods of instruction, and also will filter down from the top as the masters continue to refine their performance. However these changes are manifested, view them with gratitude rather than annoyance, for they are one of the few ways that you can see that others are working for your ultimate benefit.

1 History and Philosophy

Aikido is defined by the way which relates man to the cosmic power, or ki. This idea of man in harmony with the creative and original force of all things, is also at the root of life and serenity. 'He who discovers the secret of aiki-do,' said Master Ueshiba, 'has the universe within him and can say "I am the universe".'

Michel Random (1987)

All the present-day martial arts originated from early forms of hand-to-hand

Fig 1   'I want considerate people to listen to the voice of Aikido. It is not for correcting others; it is for correcting your own mind' (Morihei Ueshiba 1883–1969).

combat and stick-fighting techniques. These original techniques were refined over the years and developed by the practitioners of martial arts, who were themselves subject to influence by the concepts of Buddhism. Although martial arts started as collections of techniques, they outgrew the original objective of incapacitating the opponent and began to take on the deeper concept of 'ways'.

Following the demise of the Samurai class, the martial arts began to embrace the moral overtones which were linked to the daily life of society as a whole. Increasing stress was placed upon the development of fortitude and moral fibre. It is important nowadays to not lose sight of one fundamental tenet – these are the arts of fighting. They should not be treated as mere exercises in technique or spiritual training.

Aikido is thought to have its roots in Daito Aiki Jutsu, founded by Prince Teijun (850–880AD) and passed on through successive generations of the Minamoto family and the House of Takeda until 1868. It was at that time that Sokaku Takeda started teaching the art outside the family in Hokkaido where the Daito school is situated.

MORIHEI UESHIBA

The history of aikido is synonymous with the life story of Morihei Ueshiba, the founder of the art, who was born in 1883, the son of a farmer in Tanabe. He was apparently a rather weak child who was encouraged by his father, Yoroku, to take up physical activities such as sumo and swimming in order to build up his strength and stamina rather than just reading books and studying art and religion, which was said to be his preference.

In 1901 Morihei travelled to Tokyo with the intention of starting a small stationery business. During his brief stay in the city, Morihei commenced training in ju jutsu at the Kito Ryu dojo under master Tokusaburo Tojawa. He is said to have enjoyed this training and was only prevented from continuing his studies by the failure of his business and his falling ill with a severe case of beriberi, which spurred him to return to Tanabe.

In 1903 Morihei enlisted into the infantry, serving in Manchuria during the Russo-Japanese War of 1904/5, where he gained rapid promotion. His four-year term of service was completed with distinction, and he developed unusual skills at bayonet fighting and an ability to anticipate attack. These talents are not surprising with hindsight, but at the time they were regarded as quite uncanny.

During the spring of 1912 Morihei and his family moved to Hokkaido where he was to meet the Grand Master of Daito Ryu Aiki Jutsu, Takeda Sokaku, with whom he studied intensively until his return to Tanabe in 1919. Master Sokaku was an invincible man who did not teach at any permanent dojo but travelled widely, attracting disciples with his extraordinary feats of prowess. It has been said that he would permit his hands to be tied behind his back and then invite his audience to try to throw him. He would then proceed to throw each of them to the floor as they came at him. So impressed by this was Morihei that he built a dojo for Sokaku on his property in Hokkaido where he could live and teach, eventually giving it to Sokaku when he returned to Tanabe.

At this juncture in his life, Morihei became involved with the Omote Kyu religious sect which was led by Master Deguchi Onisaburo. He studied and travelled with Onisaburo through Korea, China and Manchuria until 1925, when it is said that he experienced a profound revelation.

Morihei, now in his forty-third year, went into his garden to rest one spring day. As he rested, he experienced an enlightenment as to the close connection between *budo* and love. From this moment, Morihei understood that he must blend the highest of man's ethics with the practice of martial arts. The following excerpt from *Aikido*, by his son Kisshomaru Ueshiba, outlines this experience.

. . . when I was taking a walk in the garden by myself, I felt that the universe suddenly quaked, and that a golden spirit sprang up from the ground, veiled my body, and changed my body into a golden one. At the same time my mind and body became light. I was able to understand the whispering of the birds, and was clearly aware of the mind of God, the creator of the universe. At that moment I was enlightened: the source of budo is God's love — the spirit of loving

protection for all beings. Endless tears of joy streamed down my cheeks.

In 1927, Morihei and his family moved to Tokyo where his prowess was quickly noticed and his classes filled rapidly. Many well-known martial artists trained with him at that time, including Dr Jigoro Kano, the founder and Master of Judo. His Kobukan dojo in Tokyo was successful for many years until the outbreak of World War II, which decimated his classes. His teachings were at that time conducted under the title of Ueshiba Aiki Jutsu, and he became active in the instruction of bayonet fighting at several military academies for a while.

There are many stories of Morihei's prowess during this period. At one class, he requested five of his biggest students to hold him down on the floor, one on each arm and leg and one on top of him applying a choke hold. He was seen to throw them all off without effort and very little movement. At other times his pupils would try to sneak up on him, even when he was asleep, but they could never get close unnoticed. Morihei told them that he could sense their presence whenever they approached within ten or fifteen feet, whether he was asleep or awake, which explains his earlier documented talents for anticipating attack during the Russo-Japanese war.

In 1942, Morihei and his family moved away from Tokyo to build a new dojo at Iwama, passing the custody of the Kobukan dojo to his surviving son, Kisshomaru. His life at Iwama became one of peace where he practised and farmed, and built the Aiki Shrine. It was finally here at Iwama that Aiki Jutsu was rechristened Aikido, the Way of Harmony of the Spirit, and where the techniques were honed and the philosophies

of his art recorded. Farming and aikido remained Morihei's way of life as he continued to refine his technique up until the end of his life in 1969. On 26 of April of that year Morihei Ueshiba finally succumbed to cancer of the liver, his Iwama dojo passing to Morihiro Saito, who still teaches there. Every year there is a memorial service to O Sensei (Great Teacher) at the Aiki Shrine.

AIKIDO TODAY

Aikido differs from other martial arts in its motivations and ideology as well as in its unique style of practice. It is purely a defensive art form which relies upon a reflexive reaction to neutralise an unprovoked attack. The techniques, if performed correctly, should cause no serious injury to the attacker. The goal of aikido self-defence is to neutralise an attacker with skill, blending with your opponent and control so that he or she remains uninjured. This level of skill requires intensive practice over many years, together with a strict code of ethics. Aikidoka must be dedicated to defending themselves without hurting their opponents, a high moral approach which is difficult to maintain in today's world.

The trends established in recent years have caused a divergence in the forms of aikido, more noticeably since O Sensei died. Those instructors who were taught by O Sensei have tended to base their instruction upon his traditional methods of practice where the main opponent is yourself rather than your training partner. The various schools of aikido that have developed over the years bear the names of their masters – Tomiki, Shioda, and so on – each focusing upon those aspects that their masters feel are the most important.

The reason these schools differ from one another is summed up by Shirata Sensei in *Aikido: The Way of Harmony* (John Stevens, 1984) where he explains that Ueshiba continually refined his approach and the execution of his techniques. Aikido techniques are not static but are infinitely varied responses to a particular situation. Every generation of student is exposed to a different type of aikido, and within each generation each student has his or her own interpretation of what is taught.

UNDERLYING PHILOSOPHIES

The philosophies of aikido remain somewhat obtuse and deep, reflecting the personality of the founder and his teachings. Generally, it may be said that the objective of aikido is to remove the psychological, organic and muscular obstacles created by man, which serve to hamper his training and his search for enlightenment. There is a general study of posture and respiration coupled with a concentration aimed at self-evaluation.

Underpinning the training is the development of *ki* as well as relaxation, which should promote an overall awareness within the body and a state of readiness for action without tension. The throwing techniques observe the principles of circularity, which enhances their effectiveness. A deeper understanding of these principles will make for self-accomplishment and thus a mastering of oneself, which is fundamental to the acquisition of Master status in the art.

2 The First Stages

There are really no good students or bad students of aikido.
Only those who are alive in discovery and training, and those
who are not.

Bruce Klickstein (1987)

ETIQUETTE

The etiquette practised in aikido is quite formal, as it should be in all martial arts. Without etiquette, a martial art will lose much of its charisma, which is one of the main attractions for people of the western world, and the concepts underlying the art will become removed a step further away.

The first time you enter a dojo (training hall) will mark the beginning of another world for you. As you step into the dojo you are expected to perform *tachirei* (standing bow), as you must also do when you leave it at the end of the session. Inside the dojo will be a matted area that should cover most of the floor (*see* Fig 2). One side of the mat is designated as the *shomen*, and reserved for the instructor and honoured guests. A picture of Master Ueshiba should be displayed at the centre of that side if the dojo is intended for aikido. Sometimes you will see more than one picture where the dojo is in use for other martial arts as well; for example; Dr Jigoro Kano's picture will be present where judo is practised.

Opposite the *shomen* is the *shimoza* (lower seat) where the students will line up in rank order: highest to the right, facing *shomen* (left of *shomen*). When there is an honoured guest present, the instructor will place himself on the left of *shomen*, the guest occupying the *joseki* (high seat), under Master Ueshiba's picture. (Master Ueshiba is more commonly referred to as O Sensei – Great Master – and this term will be used from here onwards.)

Fig 2 Layout of the dojo.

When you step on to the mat you must always bow in the direction of *shomen*. This standing bow (*tacherei*) extends down about 30 degrees, your fingertips sliding down the front of your thighs to the tops of your knees (*see* Fig 3). You must now wait for the instructor to start the session formally, and usually you would perform some basic warming up exercises during this time, or practise lightly with a partner.

When your instructor indicates that the class is due to begin, usually by a clap of his hands, or verbally, you take your place in line according to your grade, highest grades on the right. You sit in *seiza* (formal sitting posture) without talking. This posture involves sitting back on your heels, with your toes touching and your hands relaxed, palms down, on your thighs (as shown in Figs 4 and 5).

The ceremonial bow may take many forms, depending upon your instructor or the style of aikido practised. Whatever the form of ceremony, all students will perform *zarei* (kneeling bow) (as shown in Fig 6). Students should remain in *zarei* while the instructor turns back to the class and performs a further *zarei*. As he rises from the bow, the students will rise up into *seiza* in order of grade, progressing from the highest grades on the instructor's left, to the most junior students on the right who rise last.

Formal bowing is performed as a token of respect for the training hall, your instructor, O Sensei and one another at various times. When addressing your instructor, you should commence the interaction with *tachirei* and finish in the same fashion. When practising with another aikidoka you bow to one another before and after the practising. You also perform *tachirei* whenever you leave the mat or the dojo.

Fig 3   *Tachirei* – the standing bow.

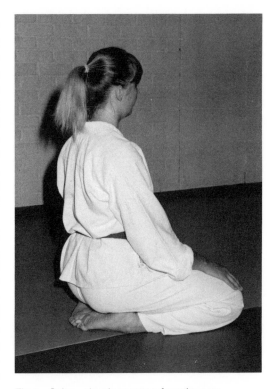

Fig 4   *Seiza* – showing posture from the rear.

17

Fig 5 *Seiza* – formal sitting position.

In addition to the formal bowing at the commencement and finish of the class, students must become familiar with certain Japanese phrases which should be used at these times:

1. When about to commence training: *Onegai shimasu*, which means 'Let us begin'.
2. When concluding the session: *Domo arigato gozaimashita*, which means 'Thank you very much'.

TERMINOLOGY

Stance and posture are extremely important in aikido training. The movements

Fig 6 *Zarei* – the kneeling bow.

18

will be demonstrated first by your instructor who will usually refer to the various postures you are to adopt in Japanese. It is, therefore, essential that you start with at least a rudimentary knowledge of the more basic terms. Here are a few of the more common Japanese terms you will probably hear, with a brief translation of each:

Stances

Ai hanmi Mutual stance, each partner in right (or left) posture facing one another.
Ai hanmi katate dori Right hand holding right wrist, both in right posture (or the converse).
Gyaku hanmi Opposite or reverse stance, partners in opposite postures to one another.
Gyaku hanmi katate dori Right hand holding left wrist, partners in opposite stances (or the converse).

Holdings

Sode dori Holding the sleeve just above the elbow.
Morote dori One wrist held by two hands.
Ryote dori Both wrists being held.
Ushiro ryote dori Both wrists held from behind.
Mune dori Front lapels being held by one hand.

Strikes

Shomen uchi Strike to the top of the head.
Yokomen uchi Strike to the side of the head.
Oi tsuki Straight blow with fist to the abdomen.

Other Terms

Hidari Left   *Migi* Right
Irimi Entering   *Tenkan* Turning
Omote Forwards   *Ura* Backwards

NB *Omote* and *ura* relate to uke (your partner).

BREAKFALLS

For those students who have previously undertaken some training in judo, the concept of breakfalling will not be unfamiliar. In its simplest form, the breakfall (*ukemi*) is the method by which you protect yourself from injury after you are thrown. In aikido, *ukemi* has been extended so that in addition to its being used for self-protection, it is also a means of preparing yourself to re-engage in combat. The finish of each *ukemi* will return you to a state of readiness, to the correct posture and awareness.

The beginner commences training in *ukemi* from a kneeling position, carefully performing forward and backward rolls before building up to full *ukemi* from a standing position. Your forward roll should not be straight but start from one arm and shoulder, and finish on the opposite hip so that you actually roll diagonally across your back instead of straight down it (as shown in Fig 7). Similarly, with the backward roll you will start on one hip and finish by rising from the opposite shoulder (as shown in Fig 8). These two basic *ukemi* are used extensively throughout aikido and other forms of *ukemi* will develop from them as you progress within your club.

It is important to remember that a rolling breakfall is intended to cover a length of the mat and should not be carried out on the spot. You should aim to roll along or across the mat and not straight down into it. Much practice is needed to be able to perform the rolls silently and smoothly.

POSTURE

Before starting aikido practice it is important to be able to adopt the correct posture. Bruce Klickstein, in his book *Living Aikido*, has said, 'In truth, there are no stances in aikido . . . however, the process of learning aikido techniques and the principles behind them requires clear static forms that give you first-hand experience of the fundamental principles being practised.'

In order to execute the techniques correctly, it is usual to adopt a triangular stance (as demonstrated in Fig 9). Such a stance has the advantage of being stable yet flexible when you may need to move quickly. To quote from *Dynamic Aikido* by Gozo Shioda,

Fig 7   *Ukemi* – the forward roll.

Fig 8   *Ukemi* – the backward roll.

'However solid a building may appear, it is worthless if its foundations have not been well laid. This is also true of the body . . . .' It is thus important to develop a firm stance upon which you may build effective technique.

Two basic stances may be adopted: *migi hanmi* (right posture) and *hidari hanmi* (left posture). For *migi hanmi*, the right foot is placed forward about one and a half times the length of your foot, toes pointing directly forwards while your left foot is at right angles to it, toes pointing to your left. About two-thirds of your weight should be on the leading leg with your right arm at chest level, elbow slightly bent. Your left hand should be about four inches in front of your stomach. Both hands should be in line with the centre of your body, fingers open and pointing forwards. Your head, neck and back should be straight with your shoulders relaxed.

This chapter has covered the basic requirements of aikido etiquette and terminology, and has outlined the basic methods for *ukemi* and *hanmi*. During your training in your club, you will have

Fig 9 *Hidari hanmi*: Correct posture and triangular stance.

many varied exercises to perform based upon *ukemi* and *hanmi* which will continue throughout your career in aikido. You must be aware that such exercises are vitally important as they help to form the foundations upon which your aikido theory will be constructed. You cannot have one without the other. Poor posture and bad *ukemi* will lead to bad aikido, which is not aikido at all.

3 Breath Control and Blending

Kokyu . . . is not mere mechanical breathing with the lungs; it is the fundamental rhythm of life that energises and fills the universe. To develop good kokyu, *we need profound insight into the nature of existence and correct application of certain principles.*

John Stevens (1984)

The principles of breath control and blending form a specialised area of aikido, which leads you towards relaxation and the subsequent development of your *ki*. The exercises detailed in this chapter will all be used at various times throughout your training. The majority of these exercises may be practised anywhere and at any time where space and your partner permit. It is important when practising them to ensure that you breathe correctly. You must inhale as you prepare for the technique and exhale as you perform the movement, controlling your exhalation of breath during this performance so that you are left with some breath at its conclusion.

The first exercise, *kokyu dosa*, is performed in *seiza* and involves the development of co-ordinated inner power. It is the basic exercise of sitting extension and will be practised for a few minutes during most lessons.

Kokyu ho, as described in this text, is an exercise where your partner holds your arm tightly with both hands. This serves to strengthen your posture and accentuate your hip movement, as well as helping with your breath control.

The basic blending exercise, *tai no henko*, trains you to absorb the power of your partner's attack. It combines breath control and blending in its initial form. When coupled with an extension of *ki*, it can progress to *kokyu nage*, a basic throwing exercise. The practice of *kokyu nage* in its various forms is the subject of a later chapter but in the following list of exercises, the extension of *tai no henko* to *kokyu nage* will be described as the one follows naturally from the other.

The exercises in this chapter are described only in their fundamental forms and can all be developed into more complex techniques as you progress over the years. This book is intended to be of help to those who are commencing training in aikido, or to those who are contemplating such training. Other books and your instructors will take you the rest of the way. It is essential to practise these exercises in conjunction with technique as they provide you with a sound basis from which to start. They form an important part of your grading syllabus as well as giving you a grounding in control and co-ordination.

Kokyu Dosa *(Fig 10)*

This exercise is practised in *seiza*, facing your partner who will grasp both your wrists (*ryote dori*) with a firm grip. Turn your hands, palm upwards, as if you were opening a book, brushing your fingertips across your partner's wrists and breathing deeply to your centre. As you start to exhale turn your hands back in a spiral towards your partner, whose elbows should rise as you extend your arms. Continue to extend your arms towards your partner, redirecting his power back into him and up towards his rear, but keeping your elbows down as you do this.

Moving from your hips, turn your partner to one side so that he falls on his back, still holding on to your wrists. Follow him on your knees (*suwari*), settling at his side with one knee braced against his body. Extend your arms towards him to pin him to the mat, maintaining circularity in your arms (as shown in Fig 10 a–f), so that he cannot rise until you permit him to do so. Your partner may push against your posture in an attempt to rise, thus testing your extension. He should be unable to move you if you are performing extension correctly.

Figs 10(a–f) *Kokyu dosa*: basic exercise of sitting extension.

Fig 10 (b)

Fig 10 (c)

Fig 10 (d)

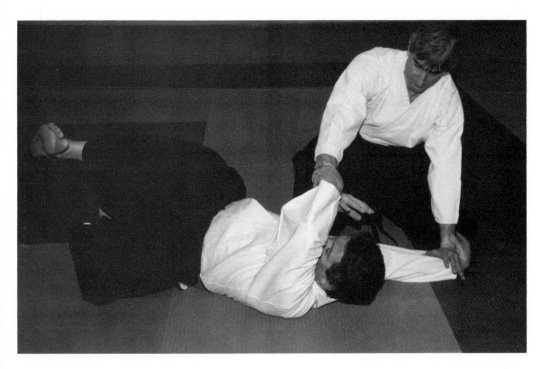

Fig 10 (e)

Fig 10 (f)

Variations of this basic exercise will occur when your partner holds your wrists from above or below, or pins your hands together or holds your elbows. These will be demonstrated in your class as you gain experience, and you need only the basic version here. Two versions other than the basic movement are illustrated in *Living Aikido* by Bruce Klickstein (1987), which provides a very detailed description of this and other exercises.

Kokyu Ho (Fig 11)

John Stevens, in his book *Aikido: The Way of Harmony*, has said that 'breath sparks life and vivifies the body; as long as our *kokyu* is deep and steady we will flourish'. *Kokyu ho* may be translated as 'breath meditation', and encompasses a wide range of exercises including *makoto no kokyu* (true breath), *ten no*

kokyu (the breath of heaven), *chi no kokyu* (the breath of earth), *jin no kokyu* (the breath of human beings) and *kokyu undo* (breath movement), of which there are several variations.

The exercise demonstrated here is called *morote dori kokyu ho*, a variation of *kokyu undo*. This exercise serves to demonstrate breath control and movement as well as providing your partner with a chance to practise *ukemi*. It is a particularly interesting exercise to practise as it also involves the demonstration of a weaker, single arm overcoming the combined power of two arms and actively throwing *uke* (your partner who takes the *ukemi*) at its conclusion.

Your partner commences by holding one of your arms with both of his hands (*morote dori*). Lower your elbow and step forwards with your right foot deeply past uke's left foot (assuming that uke is in left posture holding your right

Figs 11(a–e) *Kokyu ho*: exercise to aid posture and hip movement.

Fig 11 (b)

Fig 11 (c)

Fig 11 (d)

arm). As you bring your centre towards uke you begin to raise both your arms, bending them at the elbows and turning to face in the same direction as uke while sliding your left foot up to your right, slightly in front of uke's line. Ensure that you are close to uke, as any gaps between you can ruin the effectiveness of the technique.

Step across and behind uke with your right foot, raising your arms and keeping your right elbow across uke's chest. When you feel that uke is unbalanced, which should happen as uke is being bent backwards, turn your hips to your

Fig 11 (e)

Fig 12 (b)

Figs 12(a–e)   *Tai no henko*: exercise in control
and blending.

right and settle into right posture,
extending your arms naturally to your
right. Uke will be thrown backwards on
to the mat.

During this exercise you must breathe
in as you commence the initial entry,
breathing deeply as you raise your arms
and exhale as you change your posture
and extend to throw uke.

Tai No Henko (Fig 12)

This may be practised from a static posture or in motion (*ki no nagare*). The static
form is described first as it is the most
basic and usually is the initial form to be
taught. Partners commence by adopting
gyaku hanmi: you assume *migi hanmi*
(right posture), whilst your partner assu-
mes *hidari hanmi* (left posture), grasping

your right wrist with his left hand. You
should be standing in a relaxed manner,
shoulders lowered and hands open, feeling the energy within your body.

Breathe in as you step forwards to
meet uke toe to toe, bringing your centre
to meet uke's grip instead of trying to
pull uke's hand towards you. Easing
towards uke's gripping hand is essential
for accomplishing the technique without
the use of force.

Keeping your hand in front of your
centre, turn your hips and body to your
left, stepping back with your left foot
until you have adopted *migi hanmi*, facing in the same direction as uke with
your hands extending directly out from
your centre. Bear in mind that both of
your hands must extend forwards, palms
upwards as if you were reading a book.
Hold this posture for a few seconds
allowing your breath to continue exhaling and forcing your spirit out through

Fig 12 (c)   Fig 12 (d)

your extended hands. You should be
well balanced and in a strong posture
while uke will be bent forwards and
down in a weak position.

Kokyu Nage from Tai No Henko

Having performed the *tai no henko*
movement for some time, you will begin
to find that you can accomplish the
technique whilst uke resists, and you will
now be in a position to extend the exercise into *kokyu nage*. Perform *tai no
henko*, exhaling as you turn and extend
your hands forwards. Continue to
extend your right hand (or left hand if
this is gripped by uke) forwards and
gradually around to your left in a downward spiral, turning your palm inwards
again as you push your power forwards
through the edge of your arms. Uke will

Fig 12 (e)

follow your wrist forwards and round, finally unbalancing to perform a rolling *ukemi* forwards to return to *hidari hanmi* facing you across the mat in the ready posture.

Ki No Nagare

This is the performance of any technique in motion, but is used here to describe the movements of *tai no henko* from a flexible position. You perform the same moves as described previously as uke moves towards you, reaching for your right wrist. You should commence to move before uke can take hold and you can extend forwards from your turn to continue uke's movement into *kokyu nage* if desired. The technique is usually practised to the final posture of *tai no henko*.

If uke initially experiences difficulty in following you, permit him to grip your wrist lightly. Where you extend this into *kokyu nage* it is best practised in groups of four or five, each taking turns to be tori (the person who performs the throw) whilst the others act as a series of ukes. This leads you into the later chapter on *kokyu nage*, which covers this and other similar techniques.

These exercises and their variations are intended to provide you with the sound foundations necessary from which to extend your study of aikido technique. The extension of *tai no henko* into

kokyu nage from a flexible posture will be the beginning of the specific chapter on *kokyu nage*. John Stevens (*Aikido: The Way of Harmony*) has said, 'Aikido breathing techniques are said to purify the internal organs, stimulate the blood, and promote good health. In order to apply the aikido techniques smoothly and correctly we must be naturally linked to our partners and our environment through *kokyu* at every stage.' It is widely accepted that correct breathing is essential for all activities including sports, dancing and singing. Tuition in most sports, and other activities such as music, will usually include instruction in breath technique. This has been taken a stage further in aikido where breath control and the summoning of *ki* are closely linked. It is the learning of good breath control that encourages the development of *ki* and thereafter the beginnings of good aikido.

These are the basic prerequisites for all aikido technique and they will be reiterated throughout the book as and where necessary. Part of your mind will eventually become adapted to subconsciously checking your breathing as you perform techniques after a few years. It is at the novice stages that most difficulties concerning these concepts are encountered. Trying to remember posture, hand positions and breath control all at one time can be daunting. By way of encouragement, I can recall being totally confused for a very long time, and can still feel that confusion from time to time even now.

4 Immobilisation Techniques

In aikido, efficiency should and will result from precision of operations; it will be a natural consequence of the correct performance of the various programmed motions which are the bare bones of each technique.

A Westbrook and O Ratti (1970)

In aikido, the core of the instruction is centred around the techniques that make up the main syllabus. All styles have such techniques common to their practice, although the mode of performance may vary at times. These core techniques may be broken conveniently into two separate headings: those used for the immobilisation of an aggressor and those used to throw the opponent. In the latter case, you can often apply a pinning technique following the throw if required.

Training in these techniques follow a series of stages, called forms, and the further you progress, the more like a real-life situation the form will become. The terms 'solid' and 'flexible' are also used to describe the manner in which uke will attack. Solid refers to a situation in which uke will be stationary and holding your wrist, sleeve or collar, while the term flexible refers to uke making a grab for you or throwing a punch or strike. In other words, the flexible technique tends to reflect a true-to-life situation, whilst solid posture is intended for practice during the early stages when you are learning the essential elements of each technique.

The forms most often demonstrated in aikido clubs are as follows:

First form: *Ai hanmi katate Dori* (Fig 13) where uke grasps your right (left) wrist with his right (left) hand
Second form: *Gyaku hanmi katate Dori* (Fig 14) where uke grasps your left (right) wrist with his right (left) hand
Third Form: *Sode dori* (Fig 15) where uke grasps your left (right) upper sleeve with his right (left) hand
Fourth form: *Mune dori* (Fig 16) where uke grasps your collar (or shirt front) with his right (left) hand
Fifth form: *Shomen uchi* (Fig 17) where uke makes a strike to the top of your head with his handblade
Sixth form: *Yokomen uchi* (Fig 18) where uke makes a strike with his handblade to the side of your head
Seventh form: *Oi tsuki* (Fig 19) where uke punches with his right (left) fist to your abdomen
Formal shomen: (Fig 20) where partners stand at fighting distance with wrists crossed

These forms are illustrated in Figs 13–20, and for the purposes of this text, the

Fig 13 *Ai hanmi katate dori*: basic first form of attack.

Fig 14 *Gyaku hanmi katate dori*: basic second form of attack.

Fig 15 *Sode dori*: basic third form of attack.

Fig 16 *Mune dori*: basic fourth form of attack.

Fig 17 *Shomen uchi*: basic fifth form of attack.

33

Fig 18   *Yokomen uchi*: basic sixth form of attack.

Fig 19   *Oi tsuki*: basic seventh form of attack.

Fig 20   Formal *shomen*: solid form of *shomen uchi*.

techniques will be demonstrated in their first and second forms as well as from formal shomen posture. Other forms will be included at the end to provide guidance for the continuation of your studies. Only a limited number of forms may be covered before you become confused, and too much information is as bad as too little. The basic forms used in this book are those that are usually taught at the early stages of training and in each case it is assumed that uke is attacking or grasping with his right hand, so you need to reverse the movements for a left-handed attack.

PINNING TECHNIQUES (IMMOBILISATION)

The techniques described in this chapter can all be dangerous if performed too quickly without proper control or with any force. Take your time when practising until you reach a stage when the technique becomes purely a reaction to an attack from your partner. If you find that you need to exert more than token strength, stop, for you are obviously doing something wrong. If you continue to build up pressure upon uke's limbs you are in danger of causing injury or damage to your partner. All the immobilisation techniques involve complex wrist, hand, foot and posture movements and these must be rehearsed slowly for many months before you are familiar enough with them to speed up your technique.

Once you have successfully applied immobilisation it is essential to recognise when to ease off and allow uke to return to his feet. Once you have been taken down to the mat, the immobilisation will be applied to your arm or wrist with slowly increasing pressure until pain is felt. If you do not indicate to your partner that this point has been reached, he may continue until your elbow, wrist or shoulder becomes damaged or dislocated. The rule is that immobilisations are applied *slowly*, and as soon as you feel any pain commencing you must tap the mat with your free hand to indicate submission.

Immobilisation techniques are intended to neutralise an attack, taking your attacker to the ground and applying a suitable lock to his shoulder, elbow or wrist to pin him down effectively. If he tries to rise, you apply the immobilisation which will cause him extreme pain and thus prevent his further movement. There are five immobilisation techniques commonly in use in aikido, each called after the Japanese number system (one to five) for convenience. At this stage only the first four will be considered. The fifth, *gokyo*, is only practised by high grades because of its potential dangers.

IKKYO

Ikkyo from *Ai Hanmi Katate Dori* (*Fig 21*)

You and your partner face one another in *ai hanmi katate dori*, uke grasping your right wrist with his right hand. Turn your right hand over so that your palm is facing upwards. This movement will turn uke's arm around so that his elbow will be easily bent. Ease forwards with your right foot while extending your right arm forwards towards uke's head. Bring your left hand up to grasp uke's right elbow, thumb downwards, as

Fig 21(a–b)   *Ikkyo*: initial entry into the technique.

Fig 21 (b)

36

you take his arm over in a wide arc controlling it with both hands until his elbow is in front of your centre.

From this position you will now be able to complete the technique in one of two basic ways, *omote* or *ura*. With the former you will enter uke's space, taking the technique through him to bring him to the ground. With the latter you step behind uke turning him around you in a downward spiral. The words *omote* and *ura* may be substituted by the words *irimi* and *tenkan* in some of the older texts, but they mean the same respectively.

Omote (Irimi) (Fig 22)

Step forwards across the front of uke with your left foot, keeping your arms down in front of your centre, your left hand rotating uke's arm as your right hand leads it downwards. Your step forwards should be directed towards

uke's third point and should be long enough to bring uke down to the mat at your side – if not you may perform a short skip forwards to complete the technique.

Ura (Tenkan) (Fig 23)

To perform this version of the technique, your step forwards with your left foot must end up toe-to-toe with uke's right foot. Keeping uke's arm at your centre, step back and around with your right foot so that your turn to the right will bring uke around with your body. Lowering your posture will help to bring uke down to the mat in a spiral.

Pinning (Fig 24)

Once uke is on the mat you should kneel beside him, your left knee pressed into

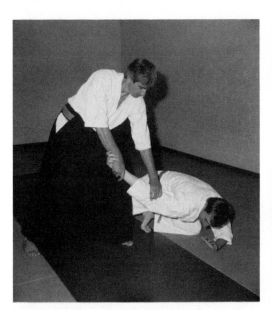

Fig 22 *Ikkyo*: 'omote' form of entry into the technique – forwards to uke's third point.

Figs 23(a–b) *Ikkyo*: 'ura' form of entry into the technique – turning uke around your posture in a downward spiral.

Fig 23 (b)

his right armpit and your right knee pushing his right forearm forwards 90 degrees from his body. Push his forearm as far forwards as possible, turning his hand over to the front. The immobilisation may be applied by pressing with your knife-hands over wrist and elbow, or by holding the elbow while bending uke's right wrist forwards and round towards his head until he taps submission.

Ikkyo from *Gyaku Hanmi Katate Dori* (*Fig 25*)

You and your partner stand in *gyaku hanmi katate dori*, uke grasping your left wrist with his right hand. Step across to your left with your left foot, applying *atemi* to uke's face with your right fist.

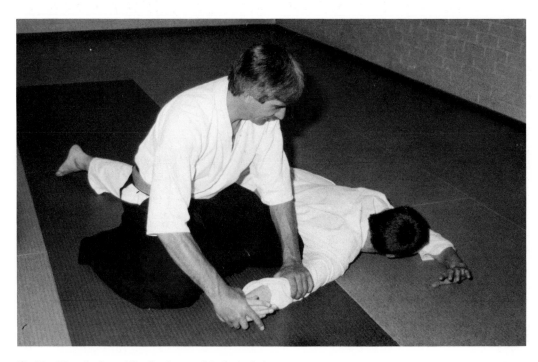

Fig 24 *Ikkyo*: the immobilisation to complete the technique.

Figs 25(a–c)   *Ikkyo*: from *gyaku hanmi katate dori*.

Fig 25 (b)   Fig 25 (c)

39

Figs 26(a–c)   *Ikkyo*: from formal *shomen*.

Fig 26 (b)

Fig 26 (c)

bring your right foot across to effect a change in posture, your right foot pointing towards uke's centre. Draw your right hand down uke's right arm to catch hold of the back of his hand. Slide your left hand to his elbow, thumb down, and step forwards with your right foot while taking uke's arm over in an arc to bring it down to a position in front of your centre.

From this position, you are now able to perform either *omote* or *ura* technique as demonstrated from first form, finishing with the immobilisation as described.

Ikkyo from *Shomen* Position (*Fig 26*)

From this posture, the technique is similar to the first form. Partners commence in formal *shomen* with right wrists crossed at fighting distance. Push your wrist forwards and upwards, grasping uke's right elbow with your left hand, thumb downwards. As you step forwards with your right foot, turn your hand over to grasp uke's right wrist and lead his arm up and over in a wide arc until you bring it down in front of your centre.

You may now step through with your left foot to make *omote* technique, or to uke's rear and around for *ura* technique, finishing with the immobilisation as described previously.

NIKKYO

Nikkyo is an extremely powerful technique which is capable of inflicting great pain upon uke if it is applied with pressure or without proper control. Practise slowly and carefully to build up speed without the use of force over a period of months.

Every person has a different threshold of pain and flexibility, and *nikkyo* will not work the same way on different individuals, so try to practise with as many partners as possible so that you can get the feel of the technique.

The technique is basically a wrist-lock applied against uke's bent arm. Once applied correctly, it then becomes a simple matter to control uke down to the mat and apply a suitable immobilisation. The secret of *nikkyo* is that you must feed back the power that uke is giving you rather than try to direct it downwards. This may sound incomprehensible at first, but it is a technique that has to be learned by experience and cannot be taught in a text such as this.

Nikkyo from *Ai Hanmi Katate Dori* (*Fig 27*)

You and your partner face each other in *ai hanmi katate dori*, uke grasping your right wrist with his right hand. Start the movement by pinning uke's right hand on to your wrist, clamping it in place with the palm of your left hand (as shown in Fig 28). Extend your right arm towards uke, sliding your wrist forwards a little through uke's grip, if possible. Extend your right hand over uke's forearm, curling it downwards towards your feet to exert pressure upon uke's wrist.

Through the technique feed uke's power back to him and lower your posture slightly to cause uke to drop at your feet. If uke does not react to the technique the fault is yours. *Do not try to force uke down.* Re-grip and try again gently until it happens. At this stage, remember that you are redirecting uke's power back through his arm and downwards.

When uke is on the mat at your feet, grasp his hand with your right and bring

Figs 27(a–d)   *Nikkyo*: from *ai hanmi katate dori*.

Fig 27 (b)   Fig 27 (c)

42

Fig 27 (d)

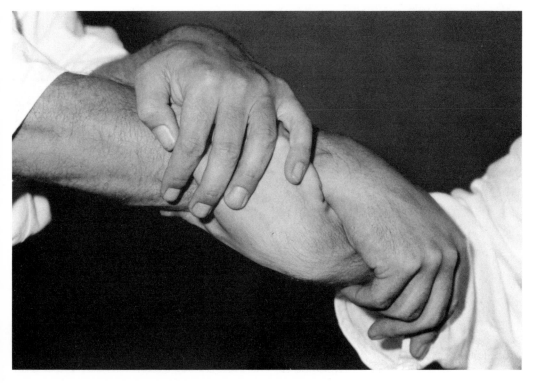

Fig 28   *Nikkyo*: first form hand position.

Fig 29   *Nikkyo* hand position for first form.

your left hand to the back of his elbow to complete the take-down by rotating uke's arm sideways and forwards.

Pinning (*Fig 30*)

Kneel into uke's side, your left knee into his right armpit and your right knee against uke's neck, bringing uke's right

arm to your left shoulder as you lower yourself into this position. Extend your left arm across uke's forearm while holding his arm against your body with your right across his elbow. Bring pressure to bear on uke's elbow by turning towards his head and extending your centre up over his back until he submits by tapping the mat. This position is important to practise carefully and if uke can roll out of it you haven't got sufficient connection to complete the pinning. It is necessary to get in as close to uke as possible and to keep your centre above his shoulder. From this position, the pin will require very little movement on your part to be effective.

Nikkyo from *Gyaku Hanmi Katate Dori* (*Fig 31*)

The application of the wrist technique in this form differs considerably from that

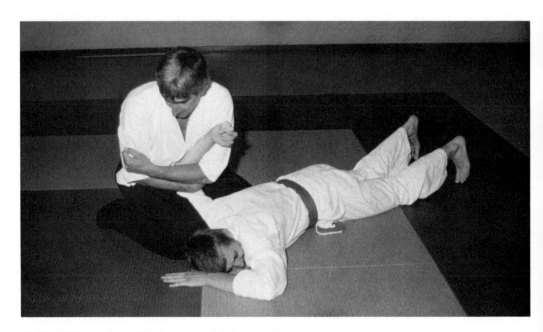

Fig 30   *Nikkyo*: the immobilisation to complete the technique.

Figs 31(a–f)   *Nikkyo*: fom *gyaku hanmi katate dori*.

Fig 31 (b)

Fig 31 (c)

Fig 31 (d)

Fig 31 (e)

Fig 31 (f)

45

Fig 31 (g)

Fig 31 (h)

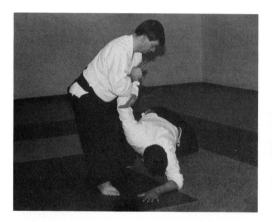

Fig 31 (i)

Fig 31 (j)

of the previous form, although the same principles underlie the technique. Start in *gyaku hanmi katate dori* with uke grasping your left wrist with his right hand. Step to your left with your left foot, drawing uke slightly off balance as you apply *atemi* with your right fist to uke's face. Slide your right foot into posture to face uke in *migi hanmi* as you slide your right hand down his arm to grasp the back of his right hand. Your left hand takes hold of uke's left elbow, thumb down, as you complete your control of uke's right arm.

Slide your left hand back over uke's forearm to grasp his wrist, pinning his

right hand against your left shoulder to augment the wrist-lock. Apply the technique by pressing his hand back against your shoulder. Bring your left foot up and slide your right foot back to change posture to *hidari hanmi*, twisting uke's forearm backwards and bending forwards slightly as you lower your posture. Uke should now drop at your feet. Bring your left hand to the back of uke's elbow to complete the take-down by rotating his arm sideways and forwards. This take-down and the subsequent immobilisation are the same as described for first form (*nikkyo* from *ai hanmi katate dori*).

Nikkyo from *Shomen Position* (*Fig 32*)

Partners commence in formal *shomen* position with right wrists crossed at fighting distance. Push your right wrist forwards and upwards, grasping uke's right elbow with your left hand, thumb down, and ease forwards on your right foot. Cut uke's arm over and down to your right as you take hold of his hand with your right hand and bring it up to

Figs 32(a–d)   *Nikkyo*: from formal *shomen*.

Figs 32 (b)

Fig 32 (c)

Fig 32 (d)

Figs 33(a–e)   *Sankyo*: from *ai hanmi katate dori*.

Fig 33 (b)

Fig 33 (c)

Fig 33 (d)

Fig 33 (e)

your left shoulder. At this point, change posture by stepping up with your left foot and back with your right foot.

Slide your left hand back over uke's forearm to grasp his wrist, pinning his right hand against your left shoulder to augment the wrist-lock. Apply the technique as in the previous description and complete with the immobilisation as detailed before.

SANKYO

The basic principle of *sankyo* is the twisting of uke's wrist inwards against

48

the joint, and the actual twisting is only practised to a slight degree during the early stages of training. As you progress through the grades, your wrists become more flexible and are able to withstand the techniques better. The early techniques are only practised sufficiently to enable you to perceive the underlying principles.

Sankyo from *Ai Hanmi Katate Dori* (*Fig 33*)

You and your partner face each other in *ai hanmi katate dori*, uke grasping your right wrist with his right hand. Your entry is the same as for the first form *ikkyo*: through uke's posture to unbalance him as you push forwards to bring his arm over and down in a wide arc. At this point, you must effect a change of hands as you step close to uke's right armpit with your left leg. Grip uke's right hand from the back with your left, your fingertips in the centre of uke's palm and your thumb over his thumb. With a slight inwards twist, you can control uke's position and cause considerable pain.

Raise your left hand and press it against your chest, turning towards uke to make *atemi* with your right fist. Cut uke's arm downwards across your body so that he is brought to his knees in front of you. Place your right hand over uke's elbow and pull him forwards and down to the mat as you step around and backwards.

Drop down to the mat with uke so that your right knee is beside his head and your left knee is into his side by his right armpit, keeping the *sankyo* alive with your left hand. Bring uke's hand up to your left shoulder and transfer hands, cutting your left arm down across uke's

Fig 34 *Sankyo*: the immobilisation to complete the technique.

shoulder to pin him in position (Fig 34). Turn your body over uke's body and around towards his head until he taps submission.

Sankyo from *Gyaku Hanmi Katate Dori* (*Fig 35*)

Partners commence in *gyaku hanmi katate dori*, uke grasping your left wrist with his right hand. Step across to your left with your left foot, applying *atemi* to uke's face with your right fist. Bring your right foot into right posture as you slide your right hand down uke's arm to grasp his right hand from the back. Slide your left hand to uke's left elbow, thumb downwards as in *ikkyo*, and enter with

49

Figs 35(a–c)   *Sankyo*: from *gyaku hanmi katate dori*.

Fig 35 (b)

Fig 35 (c)

your right foot taking uke's arm over in a wide arc down to your centre.

From this point the technique follows the same lines as the first form, changing hands and grasping his right hand in *sankyo*. Continue the movement as described previously and finish with the immobilisation.

Sankyo from *Shomen* Position

Partners commence in formal *shomen* position as described for *ikkyo* and *nik-kyo* previously. The execution of the technique follows the same pattern as the first form except that you must push upwards and forwards with your right hand to commence the technique. The actual movements and the pinning completion are exactly the same as those already described.

YONKYO

This technique incorporates a sudden, sharp pressure on the nerve centre situated on the inside of the forearm of your partner, which can be most painful if applied without care. Locating the exact spot can be very difficult and the technique is anything but easy to perform correctly. The location of this nerve centre will vary with each person and you will need a great deal of practice before you develop the sensitivity necessary to find the correct spot. Pressure is applied by using the joint at the base of your index finger (as shown in Fig 36).

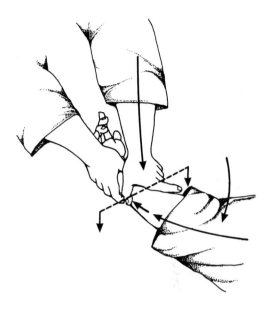

Fig 36   *Yonkyo*, application of the technique.

Yonkyo from *Ai Hanmi Katate Dori* (*Figs 37–38*)

Partners commence in *ai hanmi katate dori* and your initial entry is the same as for *ikkyo*, uke's posture being broken by cutting down with both hands on his arm to the front of your centre. Release uke's elbow and grip the inside of his wrist from above, your hand position as shown in Fig 36.

Step forwards with your left foot, applying *yonkyo* with a sword-cutting motion up, forwards and down to bring uke down to the mat. Advance your left foot to a position under uke's right shoulder and apply pressure into the shoulder joint while twisting the arm outwards until uke taps his submission (*see* Fig 38).

Yonkyo from *Gyaku Hanmi Katate Dori*

This technique is essentially the same as for the other second-form immobilisations that have already been described.

From the position where you have uke's right arm under control you proceed as detailed above.

Yonkyo from *Shomen* Position

Partners commence in formal *shomen* position as described for *ikkyo* and the other immobilisation techniques. The *yonkyo* is executed in the same fashion as the first form except that you push upwards and forwards with your right wrist to commence the technique. The immobilisation follows the same movements as described for the first form.

By the time you have learned the first and second forms, and can complete all these techniques from formal *shomen*, you will have progressed far enough not to need the guidance of a basic text such as this. For the study of techniques beyond this level I would recommend *Aikido and the Dynamic Sphere* by A.

Figs 37(a–e)   *Yonkyo*: from *ai hanmi katate dori*.

Fig 37 (b)

Fig 37 (c)

Fig 37 (d)

Fig 37 (e)

Westbrook and O. Ratti (*see* Bibliography), which provides very good diagrams and background text to many more forms than can be included here. This book is not cheap and may take time to obtain, but it will guide you through many further stages for years to come, although it differs technically from the Iwama style described in this text.

For the beginner, the best advice I can offer is not to be in any hurry to grade up. The attainment of different coloured belts can sometimes become an end in itself, an attitude which is at odds with

Fig 38 *Yonkyo*: the immobilisation to complete the technique.

the principles of the art. The way of aikido embraces the spirit of peace and love without which your practice would become worthless. To quote Morihiro Saito, 'The more present-day *budo* seeks a real peace and proves the spirit of universal love, the more severe the process should be to attain these goals. That is the world of *budo*.' This may well appear to be a contradiction in terms to many, and if you have not experienced this, it is difficult to understand. I have been through the mill myself, and I can vouch for the truth in his words.

5 Projection Techniques

. . . to learn and understand anything, you must see the whole, not just a part. There is something in aikido for everyone. All groups can benefit . . .

Martial Arts of the Orient
Ed. Bryn Williams (1987)

The words chosen to introduce this chapter have many implications for beginners and advanced aikidoka alike. Aikido training covers a wide variety of diverse methods and techniques which, unlike judo or karate, may appear to be quite unrelated at the beginning. Aikido tuition is usually given in a holistic fashion, mixing *bokken* and *jo* with immobilisation and projection techniques and *kokyu nage* in one single lesson. This is done for a reason – to underline the fact that they are all related and that you can develop one from the other – but at first it can all appear confusing. Your instructor is trying to get you to look at the whole, rather than at any specific part. You may particularly enjoy using the *bokken* or the *jo* or practising *kokyu nage* and, given the choice, would concentrate upon these areas, but you would then cease to be practising aikido.

In this book, I have deliberately divided aikido into its component parts, and concentrated upon each part in a different chapter. This is because I well remember my confusion when I first started. I was already a high-grade in judo. It took me over two years to sort it out (Perhaps this was a disadvantage).

However, this compartmentalising of aikido seems to me to be necessary for those starting to learn the art, or with an interest in finding out about it.

Probably the most spectacular part of aikido, and the area that offers the most universal appeal, is the syllabus of projection techniques. These techniques show just what aikido is capable of accomplishing and a display of these throws will often attract participants. This syllabus at basic level contains five techniques which must be studied. As with the pinning techniques, the various forms should be practised to the right and left.

SHIHO NAGE (FOUR DIRECTION THROW)

Bruce Klickstein describes *shiho nage* as the practice of infinite mobility – being able to move with ease from any direction to any other direction. He states, 'When the difference between directions disappears, you move like the radiance of the sun, emanating equally in all directions.' As you will no doubt gather from this, *shiho nage* may be performed to any direction that you may choose,

Figs 39(a–d) *Shiho nage*: from *ai hanmi katate dori*.

Fig 39 (b)

Fig 39 (c)

Fig 39 (d)

providing that you do the technique correctly to start with, and it is with this basic proviso that we are concerned here.

Shiho Nage from Ai Hanmi Katate Dori (Fig 39)

Commence with uke grasping your right wrist with his right hand in *ai hanmi*

katate dori. Step a little to your right, pushing your right arm out towards uke's weak direction (third point) to unbalance him while delivering *atemi* with your left fist to uke's side. Slide your left hand along uke's right arm to grasp the back of his right hand, thumb over and into the palm of his hand.

Move your left elbow forwards under uke's right arm, gripping his right hand

Figs 40(a–c) *Shiho nage*: from *gyaku hanmi katate dori*.

Fig 40 (b)

with both of your hands. Raise your arms, keeping your elbows level, until uke is completely unbalanced (if uke is smaller than you, you will need to lower your posture as you do this). Keep uke's elbow over your arm and your hand grip in front of your forehead. Step forwards under uke's arm with your left foot and turn your body to your right to reverse the direction in which you are facing. You should endeavour to keep your grip in front of your forehead during this turn because if it falls back to your rear, the technique will be negated.

You are now in a position to throw uke by cutting downwards with both hands towards uke's third point (where

you should now be facing). Make sure that you perform this final cut carefully as too forceful a movement could cause injury to uke at this stage.

Shiho Nage from Gyaku Hanmi Katate Dori (Fig 40)

You and your partner commence in *gyaku hanmi katate dori* with uke gripping your left wrist with his right hand. Step across to your left with your left foot and slide your right foot into right posture, aligning your right foot with uke's front foot. Reach over your left wrist to grasp uke's right wrist with your right hand.

Fig 40 (c)

Raise both your hands together and complete the technique as described for the previous application of *shiho nage.*

Remember that it is important to keep your hands in front of your forehead so as not to lose the technique as you turn.

Figs 41(a–f)   *Shiho nage*: from formal *shomen*.

Fig 41 (b)

Fig 41 (c)

Fig 41 (d)

Fig 41 (e)

Fig 41 (f)

58

Shiho Nage from *Shomen* Position (*Fig 41*)

This posture may be practised from a solid stance for beginners, partners commencing in *ai hanmi* with wrists crossed at fighting distance. As you gain experience the technique becomes more flexible where uke performs *shomen uchi* or just brings his hand up to meet yours.

As uke's right hand meets yours, allow it to push your hand down to your left, grasping his wrist from above with your left hand and applying *atemi* to uke's face with your right fist as you pull uke off balance. As uke blocks your *atemi*, grasp his right wrist with both hands easing forwards with your right foot and thrusting forwards and upwards with both hands. Step forwards with your left foot and turn your posture to your right in a complete turn to apply *shiho nage* and finish in the manner described previously.

KOTE GAESHI (WRIST TURN OUT)

This technique is an excellent example of how the person performing the throw can generate a great amount of power while expending very little energy. Simply by turning uke's wrist to the outside you can break his posture and bring him effectively to the mat. When practising this technique, be very careful not to use any more than token strength as it can inflict much pain and possible injury.

Kote Gaeshi from *Ai Hanmi Katate Dori* (*Fig 42*)

This technique has been described from a solid posture, but it can be performed

Figs 42(a–e)   *Kote gaeshi*: from *ai hanmi katate dori*.

Fig 42 (b)

Fig 42 (c)

Fig 42 (d)

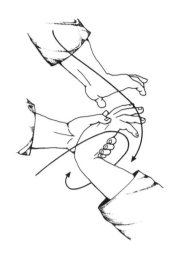

Fig 43 *Kote gaeshi* application.

Fig 42 (e)

from a flexible stance as you begin to gain more experience. You and your partner commence in *ai hanmi katate dori* with uke holding your right wrist with his right hand. Enter with your left foot to a point beside uke's front foot, at the same time turning your right hand palm upwards, to expose uke's wrist to you. Grasp uke's right wrist and lower hand with your left hand, your fingers into the lower palm of uke's hand.

Step back and around with your right

foot while removing your right hand from uke's grip. As you turn, your rotation will unbalance uke and propel him around you. At this point you may apply *atemi* with your right fist to uke's face.

Keeping your grip on uke's wrist tight into your centre, you now reverse your direction by stepping back and around with your left foot. Place your right hand on to the back of uke's right hand (Fig 43) and as you turn to your left, twist his right wrist and hand backwards and outwards. Uke will fall to the mat backwards or make a forward breakfall high over the top depending upon how the technique has been applied.

Kote Gaeshi from Gyaku Hanmi Katate Dori (Fig 44)

Commence with uke holding your left wrist in his right hand adopting *gyaku hanmi* posture. Enter by sliding your left foot forwards and then bring your right hand up between uke's hand and your arms (Fig 45), grasping his right arm as you extract your left hand from his grip. When you have your left hand free, bring

Figs 44(a–d) *Kote gaeshi*: from *gyaku hanmi katate dori*.

Fig 44 (b)

Fig 44 (c)

Fig 44 (d)

uke's right arm down and grasp his right wrist with your left hand, pivoting to your right and applying *atemi* to uke's face with your right fist.

Place your right hand on to the back of uke's right hand and begin to step back and around with your left foot, reversing your direction. Complete the technique in the same manner as was described for *ai hanmi katate dori* above.

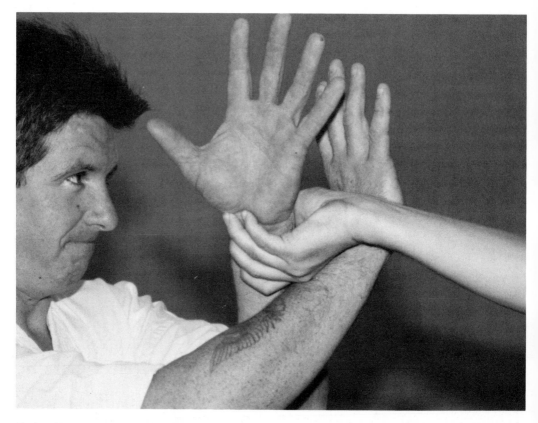

Fig 45 *Kote gaeshi*: hand position for second form release.

Kote Gaeshi from *Shomen* Position (*Fig 46*)

Once again, this is described from a solid posture but can be adapted to a more flexible stance as you progress. As your right wrists meet, step forwards with your left foot, blending with uke's movement while reaching up with your left hand to control uke's further movement. Gripping uke's right wrist with your left hand, step back around with your right foot and apply *atemi* to uke's face with your right fist. Transfer your right hand to the back of uke's right hand and reverse your direction by stepping back and around with your left foot.

Complete the technique in the same manner as described previously.

IRIMI NAGE (ENTERING THROW)

This projection technique can be accomplished from a variety of positions and it has been nicknamed the 'twenty-year technique'. After many years of practice, you will begin to see why. The projection consists of leading uke around you in one direction and then reversing your direction so that uke is brought down flat on his back on the mat. It is essential to keep the leading

Figs 46(a–e)   *Kote gaeshi*: from *shomen* posture.

Fig 46 (b)

Fig 46 (c)

Fig 46 (d)

movement throughout your reversal of direction smooth and circular so that you avoid any conflict of force.

Irimi Nage from *Ai Hanmi Katate Dori* (*Fig 47*)

Commence with uke holding your right wrist in his right hand in the solid form, or reaching for it in the more flexible form. Step with your left foot as far round behind uke's right foot as you can, at the same time blending with uke's stance so that you finish standing square to his rear with your hips aligned with

Fig 46 (e)

Figs 47(a–e) *Irimi nage*: from *ai hanmi katate dori*.

Fig 47 (b)

Fig 47 (c)

Fig 47 (d)

Fig 47 (e)

his. Pin uke's head on to your right shoulder with your left hand.

Pivot on your left foot, taking your right leg back around to your right rear, your right arm leading uke out and around you. Raise your right arm to lead uke's head and body upwards and then backwards, taking him over and down on to the mat. As you take uke over, you should step through with your right foot behind uke and project him across the mat into a backward rolling breakfall or a high fall around your hips.

Figs 48(a–c)   *Irimi nage*: from *gyaku hanmi katate dori.*

Fig 48 (b)

Irimi Nage from *Gyaku Hanmi Katate Dori* (*Fig 48*)

You and your partner commence in *gyaku hanmi* with uke holding your left wrist with his right hand. Enter with your left foot bringing your right hand up under uke's grip to break his hold (as in Fig 45). As you free your left hand, continue your entry around behind uke extending your right arm across uke's front.

The technique may now be completed in exactly the same manner as for the previous one, with uke being thrown across the mat in either a backward rolling breakfall or a high fall.

Irimi Nage from *Shomen* Position (*Fig 49*)

This technique may be performed from a solid posture as described here, or it may be practised as a flexible technique. The movements are essentially the same for both variations.

As your right wrists meet, maintain a

Fig 48 (c)

forward extension by stepping forwards with your right foot and deeply around uke with your left foot so that you finish in a posture directly behind uke. Keep uke's left arm extended by maintaining contact with your right hand throughout your entry.

The throw may now be completed in exactly the same manner as for the previous *irimi nage* techniques.

TENCHI NAGE (HEAVEN AND EARTH THROW)

This technique consists of unbalancing uke to one side and then extending through him to project him towards the other side. Your arms perform the upward and downward movements – described as reaching for heaven and earth simultaneously – one arm leading uke down while the other directs uke upwards and backwards.

Tenchi Nage from Ai Hanmi Katate Dori (Fig 50)

Commence in *ai hanmi* with uke grasping your right wrist with his right hand in the solid posture, or reaching for it in

Figs 49(a–d) *Irimi nage*: from formal *shomen*.

Fig 49 (b)

Fig 49 (c)

Fig 49 (d)

Figs 50(a–d) *Tenchi nage*: from *ai hanmi katate dori*.   Fig 50 (b)

Fig 50 (c)   Fig 50 (d)

the more flexible variation of the first form. You will need to control uke's right arm with your left hand and so you must first free your right hand before this can be done.

Turn your right hand so that your palm is towards uke, with the fingers pointing down and to the right; take hold of uke's right hand with your left hand, your fingertips in the centre of uke's palm. Enter with your left foot, turning your right hand over, palm downwards, and extending it to the right away from uke's grasp. At the same time, turn your left hand palm downwards and extend your left arm in front

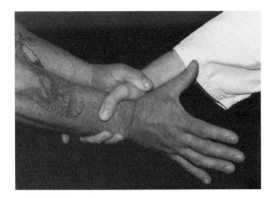

Figs 51(a–b) *Tenchi nage*: first form hand release.

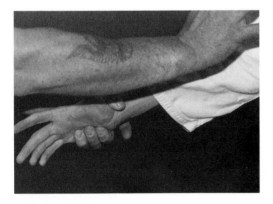

Fig 51 (b)

of your centre as you make your entry. This will give you control of uke's right arm (*see* Fig 51).

Push uke's right arm downwards and around to his rear third point as you step forwards with your left foot, unbalancing uke towards his right rear corner. As you do this, bring your right hand up towards uke's face for *atemi* and extend it up past his left cheek.

Bring your right foot up to beside your left and extend it forwards and across behind uke as you complete the extension of both your arms upwards and downwards. Your extension, coupled

with your power as you step across behind uke, is sufficient to propel him across the mat diagonally to your right.

Tenchi Nage from *Gyaku Hanmi Katate Dori* (*Fig 52*)

This is probably the simplest form of this technique and may be used as the introduction to the throw. Partners commence in *gyaku hanmi* with uke holding your left wrist with his right hand. Step forwards with your left foot, pushing uke's right arm downwards and around to his rear third point. This serves to unbalance uke towards his right rear corner in preparation for the application of the full technique.

As you bring your right foot up to your left make *atemi* by extending your right fist upwards to uke's face. Complete the technique as in the previous demonstration for first form.

Figs 52(a–c) *Tenchi nage*: from *gyaku hanmi katate dori*.

Fig 52 (b)

Tenchi Nage from *Shomen* Position (*Fig 53*)

This is described from a solid posture because the flexible one is different and not relevant here. Commence in solid posture for formal *shomen*, right wrists crossed at a fighting distance. Step forwards with your left foot, bringing your left hand up to grasp uke's right wrist as you extend your right wrist forwards and upwards. Sweep uke's right arm down in a wide arc with your left hand controlling its passage, and extend it downwards and around towards his rear third point to unbalance him to his right rear corner.

You may now complete the throw in exactly the same manner as described in the previous two examples.

KAITEN NAGE (ROTARY THROW)

This technique projects uke away from you and across the mat rather than down

Fig 52 (c)

Figs 53(a–c)   *Tenchi nage*: from *shomen* posture.

69

Fig 53 (b)

Fig 53 (c)

Figs 54(a–e) *Kaiten nage*: from *ai hanmi katate dori*.

to the ground. There are several different ways to perform the technique and you can use inner and outer spiral entries to most forms. The methods described here are the most basic forms of the throw.

Kaiten Nage from Ai Hanmi Katate Dori (Fig 54)

The simplest method for this technique consists of an entry similar to the one you would perform for *ikkyo*. Commence in *ai hanmi* with uke grasping your right wrist with his right hand. Enter by stepping forwards with your right foot, pushing upwards with your right hand towards uke's head. Slide your left hand under uke's right elbow to prevent him from countering and take uke's arm over and down in a wide circular motion finishing almost at mat level.

At this point you must change hands so that your left hand has control of uke's right arm – the grip is shown in Fig 55. With your right hand, cut uke's head in towards your centre. You could use your right knee to make *atemi* if the

Fig 54 (b)

Fig 54 (c)

Fig 54 (d)

Fig 54 (e)

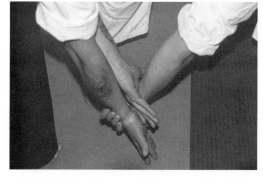

Fig 55 *Kaiten nage*: hand positions.

attack were for real at this point. Bring uke's right arm up behind his back and rotate your hips to your right as you step forwards with your left foot to project uke away from you into a rolling break-fall.

Kaiten Nage from *Gyaku Hanmi Katate Dori*

For this form, I have divided the technique into two basic methods: inner and outer spirals.

71

Figs 56(a–e) *Kaiten nage*: inner spiral.   Fig 56 (b)

Fig 56 (c)   Fig 56 (d)

Fig 56 (e)

Inner Spiral *(Fig 56)*

Commencing in *gyaku hanmi*, uke grasps your left wrist with his right hand. Lead uke's right hand to your left, stepping forwards with your left foot while extending your right handblade into uke's right elbow in an upward direction and stepping through under uke's right arm with your right foot. Turn to your left until you are facing in the same direction as uke.

Cut down to the mat with your left hand and step back with your left foot as the cut reaches low level. Apply your

Figs 57(a–d)   *Kaiten nage* outer spiral.

Fig 57 (b)

Fig 57 (c)

Fig 57 (d)

right hand to the back of uke's neck or head to cut his head to your centre. Complete the throw as in the previous description.

Outer Spiral *(Fig 57)*

Commence in *gyaku hanmi* with uke grasping your left wrist with his right hand. Step to uke's right side with your left foot, making *atemi* with your right fist to uke's face while you cut upwards and forwards with your left hand, turning it to gain control of his right arm. Continue pushing uke's arm forwards with your handblade and over in a wide arc through his posture and down towards the mat. As your left hand reaches its lowest point you cut uke's head in to your centre with your right

73

Figs 58(a–d) *Kaiten nage*: from formal *shomen*.   Fig 58 (b)

Fig 58 (c)   Fig 58 (d)

handblade. Turn to your right and step forwards with your left foot as you bring uke's arm up over his back to throw him in a forward rolling breakfall away from you.

Kaiten Nage from Shomen Position (*Fig 58*)

As before, the technique is described from a solid posture. Flexible technique may be applied but the actual movement will be different from this description.

Push forwards and upwards with your right wrist against uke's right wrist, raising your left hand to place it under uke's right elbow. Step forwards with your right foot and cut uke's arm down with both hands to a position in front of your centre but low down towards the mat. Slide your left hand down to grasp uke's wrist and complete the technique in the same manner as before.

In this chapter, you have been introduced to the five projection techniques which are most commonly taught in aikido. Unfortunately, it has not been possible to describe them in the multitude of other forms that may be practised. Most of the more advanced forms will be variations of the descriptions presented here, and examples of these are included in Chapter 9 along with other more advanced techniques.

When practising these techniques, it is important to try to perform them unhurriedly and without pauses or jerks. Smooth flowing technique not only looks good but is also kinder to your partner who has to perform breakfall at the finish. As I have stated previously, this text has been compiled as an introduction and an overall picture of aikido and, as such, it concentrates on the elements of technique which should be required at your initial gradings. More advanced techniques, whilst making interesting reading, will tend to confuse the beginner at this stage, and so they have only been touched upon in Chapter 9. What you have in this chapter is, I hope, the basis from which to expand your study of projection techniques.

6 Introduction to *Bokken*

The practice of the art of aikido . . . becomes a harmonious interaction between two or more people, fulfilling Master Ueshiba's intention via translation of the highest ethics of the East (and the West as well) into vital and active modes of conduct.

Westbrook and Ratti (1970)

THE *KATANA*

The *katana*, the traditional Japanese sword, is a weapon of superb quality, individually fashioned by specialist craftsmen for the Samurai. These weapons can be worth a great deal of money nowadays and a special Japanese society exists for the conservation of swords of beauty. Aikido is by no means the only martial art form which uses the *katana*. Others are:

Iai do: The art of drawing the sword
Tameshi giri: The art of cutting with the sword
Kendo: The art of Japanese fencing

The movements and techniques taught in aikido are all linked to the way of the sword: the completion of most projection techniques is complementary to cutting with the *katana*, and the hip and body movements and posture are all complementary to sword techniques.

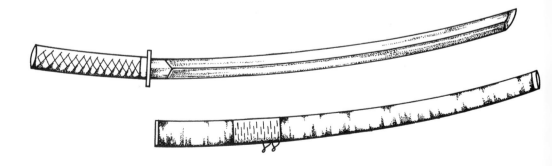

Fig 59   The *Katana*.

Whilst this relationship is very important, and it becomes more noticeable as you progress, it will not be over-emphasised at this stage. It is enough to bear in mind that this relationship exists; it will no doubt be brought to your attention during practice at your club. The sword techniques described in this chapter are basically those taught in Iwama-style traditional aikido, and other styles may differ, to a greater or lesser degree.

THE *BOKKEN (KEN)*

The *bokken* is a wooden practice sword of similar dimensions and approximate weight as the *katana*, fashioned from hard, Japanese oak. It is stout and dense so it can do considerable damage to you if contact is made. It is, however, far less intimidating than a live blade and may be used for extensive practise without anyone suffering much damage providing that it is treated carefully. Your *bokken* comes complete with a plastic *tsuba* and a rubber retaining *habaki*, but generally aikidoka tend not to fit these extras as they render the *bokken* difficult to store away.

The *bokken* has been used in place of the *katana* in competitions for many years, thus ensuring a reduction in the number of serious injuries and fatalities. Now it is used extensively as a training aid in many disciplines including aikido. The sword exercises practised in aikido during the early years of your training will be confined to the basics of *suburi* (individual practice of the various cuts and thrusts), *awase* (blending exercises) and *kumi tachi* (the set partner exercises), which precede actual free-fighting.

The importance of studying these

Fig 60   5th *kumi tachi*.

Fig 61   *Ken no kamae*: basic posture for practice with *bokken* or sword.

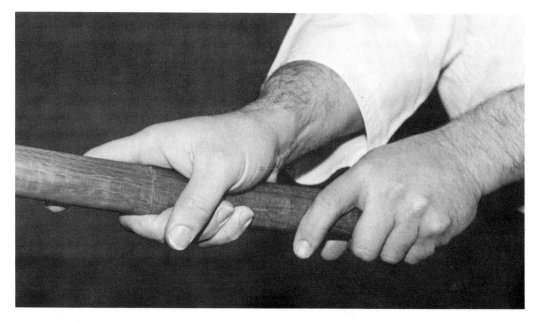

Fig 62 Gripping the *bokken*.

sword movements is that the movement of your body during the practice forms the basis for all the throwing techniques. Sword practise is fundamental to movement in aikido and the whole must be studied to be able to demonstrate the art properly. In addition to the sword techniques described, there is also a section devoted to defences against the sword, which forms an essential part of your basic technique.

POSTURE (*KAMAE*) AND GRIP

As in all aikido technique, prior to *bokken* practice it is customary to check your posture. The correct posture for work with the *bokken* is called *ken no kamae* (Fig 61), where your head, spinal column and lower abdomen are maintained in vertical alignment. The triangular stance (*hanmi*) is required for all aikido practice as it has the potential for mobility as well as promoting relaxation.

The *bokken* should be held with a firm but relaxed grip (as shown in Fig 62). Put your little finger on to the handle first, followed by each finger in turn and finishing with your thumb. Your forefingers should be relaxed in order to guide the *bokken*. Direct the tip of the *bokken* towards your imaginary partner's throat or eyes, holding it a few inches from your body in *migi hanmi*. Your right hip should be forwards and your left hand aligned with the forearm.

KEN SUBURI TECHNIQUES

These are the seven basic cutting, thrusting and moving techniques which are employed in the use of the *katana*. They will form the bulk of your *bokken* practice during the early stages of your training, as it is only when you can perform these *suburi* correctly that you can progress through the blending exercises (*awase*) to *kumi tachi*. The *suburi* are

78

Figs 63(a–c) *Shomen uchi*: the first *ken suburi*.

Figs 63(a–c) *Shomen uchi*: the first *ken suburi*.

essential to the practice of aikido as it cannot be properly combined with the sword movements if you are not competent in performing them.

When practising the *suburi*, they must be performed with full extension of your *ki* and controlled breathing. You must inhale as you raise your *bokken* and then demonstrate a controlled expellation of breath as you perform the cut or thrust. Your exhalation should be audible to your instructor and may be accompanied by a *kiai* (a piercing shout which produces an explosive outpouring of vital energy).

First *Ken Suburi – Shomen Uchi* (Fig 63)

Commence in *ken no kamae* as described on page 78. Turn your right hip back and extend your left hand forwards so that your *bokken* rises up. Swing the weapon up in a straight line over the

Fig 63 (b)

Fig 63 (c)

79

Figs 64(a–c) *Shomen uchi komi*: the second *ken suburi*.

centre of your head until your right hand is above the crown of your head. The tip of the *bokken* should now be extended down the centre of your back.

Gripping the *bokken* firmly with both hands while keeping your elbows as close together as possible in front of your head, relax your shoulders. Pull your elbows and hands downwards so that the *bokken* travels in a straight arc over your head and down to its original position. Push the weapon downwards as it swings forwards while turning your right hip forwards again, extending your right foot to the front.

This particular *suburi*, although relatively simple in application, is the essence for all the other *suburi*. It should be practised repeatedly and as often as possible to ensure both familiarity and correctness of your technique. If you cannot perform the first *suburi* correctly, the rest will become worthless.

Second *Ken Suburi* – *Shomen Uchi Komi* (Fig 64)

As with the first *suburi*, commence in *ken no kamae*. Start to raise your *bokken*

Fig 64 (b)

Fig 64 (c)

while stepping backwards with your right foot as your hands reach head level. Extend the *bokken* upwards and to your rear above your head, pausing for a second. Gripping the *bokken* firmly, draw it downwards, bringing your right hand to the crown of your head as in the first *suburi*. Step forwards with your right foot as you cut in *shomen uchi* straight down and forwards. Your right hip turns forwards as the *bokken* descends to the front of your centre, as in the first *suburi*.

This *suburi* is essentially the same as the first with the exception that your right foot is more mobile. It forms the first movement of the sixth and seventh *suburi*, which entail forward stepping combined with cutting and thrusting.

Third *Ken Suburi* – The Sword of Universal *Ki* (*Fig 65*)

From *ken no kamae*, commence by raising your *bokken* and stepping back with your right foot as you did in the second *suburi*. This time the *bokken* is extended vertically above your head, pointing towards the sky with your arms pushing it up as far as it will go. Your hips should be square with your posture as you inhale deeply through your nose. You are drawing the *ki* from the universe down through your *bokken* and into your centre.

When your lungs are full, drop your *bokken* slowly to your right side, compressing your breath to your centre while

Figs 65(a–e) Sword of universal *ki*: the third *ken suburi*.

Fig 65 (b)

81

Fig 65 (c)

looking forwards towards your imaginary adversary and turning your body into correct posture. As your *bokken* reaches a position level with your centre, turn your body to the front, bringing the *bokken* up so that your right hand is over the crown of your head, relaxed and ready to strike. Step forwards with your right foot and cut with *shomen uchi*, expelling your breath with a long drawn-out *kiai*.

Every time you practise the *suburi*, especially this particular one, the cut should be carried out with total commitment – as if you were faced with an adversary whom you must kill in order to survive. I must mention here the distinction between commitment and aggression. Aggression is an emotive force that may override commitment, whereas commitment implies full self-control during the technique. Thus you must make the cuts meaningfully but without the involvement of aggression which could mar your technique. It is better to practise five *suburi* with full commitment than five hundred without spirit.

Fig 65 (d)

Fig 65 (e)

Figs 66(a–d) *Renzoku shomen uchi komi*: the fourth *ken suburi*.

Fig 66 (b)

Fig 66 (c)

Fig 66 (d)

Fourth *Ken Suburi – Renzoku Shomen Uchi Komi (Fig 66)*

This is the first of the *suburi* that are completed on the move. Essentially, it is a series of *shomen uchi* cuts performed as you walk forwards, cutting while in right and left postures alternately. You

should practise this *suburi* until you are familiar with it as it forms the basis for the fifth to seventh *suburi*.

Commence in *ken no kamae*, raising your *bokken* straight upwards and back over your head in *shomen uchi* (first *suburi*). Perform the first *suburi*, stepping forwards with your right foot to

Figs 67(a–i) *Renzoku shomen uchi komi*: the fifth *ken suburi*.   Fig 67 (b)   Fig 67 (c)

complete the technique. You now raise your *bokken* again, advancing your centre forwards over your right foot while stepping forwards with your left foot. At this point, your hips are still in right posture. As you cut with your left foot forwards, your left hip turns forwards as you assume left posture.

Raise your *bokken* once again, advancing your weight on to your leading left foot before stepping forwards with your right, your hips remaining in left posture. Cut with *shomen uchi* as you turn your hips back into right posture. Continue this sequence until you are familiar with the movements.

Fifth *Ken Suburi – Renzoku Shomen Uchi Komi* (Fig 67)

Whilst essentially similar to the previous *suburi*, the fifth *suburi* involves the additional movement of raising the *bokken* to provide head protection between strikes. Care must be taken not to stand or approach too close to other aikidoka

during this practice as this *suburi* incorporates sideways movement of the *bokken*.

Commence from *ken no kamae*, and perform the second *suburi* as described. From this point, advance your weight on to your leading right foot while raising both your hands to a position in front of and slightly above your head. The *bokken* should be horizontal and pointing to your right. As you step forwards with your left foot swing the *bokken* round to your rear while drawing your right foot into a triangular position behind your left foot (pointing to your right). Cut with *shomen uchi* as you turn your hips into left posture.

Holding your hips in left posture you now step forwards with your right foot, raising the *bokken* to the defensive position in front of and slightly above your head. This time your wrists are crossed as the *bokken* now points towards your left. Swing the *bokken* around to your rear, drawing your left foot to the triangular position behind your right foot and cut with *shomen uchi* as your hips turn into right posture. Repeat this sequence as you progress along the mat.

Fig 67 (d)   Fig 67 (e)   Fig 67 (f)

Fig 67 (g)   Fig 67 (h)   Fig 67 (i)

Sixth *Ken Suburi – Shomen Uchi Tsuki (Fig 68)*

This and the final *suburi* introduce a further element into the sequence – thrusting. By design, the Japanese sword is not primarily a piercing weapon, but one designed to cut along the length of its blade. The tip is, however, honed to a point and it will thrust to good effect when required.

Commence in *ken no kamae* where you perform *shomen uchi komi* (second *suburi*). From this position, slide your right foot forwards, turning your right hip further forwards and thrusting

Figs 68(a–h)   *Shomen uchi tsuki*: the sixth *ken suburi*.

Fig 68 (b)

Fig 68 (e)

Fig 68 (f)

Fig 68 (c)

Fig 68 (d)

Fig 68 (g)

Fig 68 (h)

straight to your imaginary adversary's abdomen. The cutting edge of the *bokken* should be turned in the direction of your hips (to your left in this case).

You should now perform left *shomen uchi komi* as in the fifth *suburi* and from that position, slide your left foot forwards, turning your left hip further forwards as you thrust the *bokken* towards the abdomen of your imaginary adversary. The cutting edge should now be turned to your right.

Repeat this sequence as you progress along the mat.

Seventh *Ken Suburi – Migi Shomen Uchi Hidari Tsuki* (Fig 69)

In this *suburi*, you are making the cut as in the previous *suburi*, but the thrust is executed in the opposite stance each time. Thus you will only cut in *migi hanmi* and thrust in *hidari hanmi*.

Starting from *ken no kamae*, perform *shomen uchi komi* (second *suburi*). From this position, step forwards into *hidari hanmi*, turning your hips and the *bokken*'s cutting edge to your right. Thrust the *bokken* forwards towards your imaginary adversary's abdomen to complete the technique. Repeat *migi shomen uchi* and *hidari tsuki* as you progress along the mat.

These *suburi* form the basis for all sword practice within the Iwama style of traditional aikido, although they may not be the same as those practised in other schools of swordsmanship. Once you have mastered the movements described to a reasonable standard, you will be ready to progress to the partner exercises. The following two simple partner

Figs 69(a–h) *Migi shomen uchi hidari tsuki*:
the seventh *ken suburi*.

Fig 69 (b)

Fig 69 (c)

Fig 69 (d)

Fig 69 (e)

Fig 69 (f)

Fig 69 (g)

Fig 69 (h)

Figs 70(a–c) *Migi no awase*: right blending practice.

Fig 70 (b)

exercises will enable you to obtain experience of facing an adversary and blending with his attack. These exercises are expected to be performed with careful and precise technique, and while breathing correctly. *Bokken* to *bokken* contact should not happen except by accident.

AWASE (BLENDING PRACTICE)

Migi No Awase – Right Blending Practice (Fig 70)

Partners face one another in *ken no kamae*, right posture with *bokken* tips crossed. Your partner begins to raise his *bokken* to perform the first *suburi*, which will be aimed at your centre. He

Fig 70 (c)

will make *shomen uchi* cut so that it will make contact with you if you do not move.

As your partner raises his *bokken*, you must raise yours as well to perform the first *suburi*. As your partner commences his *shomen uchi* you step to your right and forwards with your right foot as you commence *shomen uchi* in harmony with your partner. Your left foot follows into *migi hanmi* as you cut down to uke's centre, ensuring that no contact is made. Pause for two or three seconds whilst maintaining *zanshin* (the spirit of the cut).

The important points for this exercise are the correctness of your first *suburi*, proper posture both before and after the cut and your breathing. Inhale as you raise your *bokken* and exhale as you cut to uke's centre.

Hidari No Awase – Left Blending Practice (Fig 71)

Partners face one another in *ken no kamae*, right posture with sword tips crossed. Your partner raises his *bokken* to perform the first *suburi*, which will be aimed at your centre. He will perform the *shomen uchi* cut to make contact with you if you do not move.

As your partner raises his *bokken*, you must raise yours to perform the first *suburi*. As your partner commences his *shomen uchi*, step to your left with your left foot, commencing *shomen uchi* in harmony with your partner. Your right foot follows into *hidari hanmi* as you cut down to uke's centre, ensuring that no contact is made. Pause for two or three seconds while maintaining *zanshin*.

Figs 71(a–c) *Hidari no awase*: left blending practice.

Fig 71 (b)

Fig 71 (c)

KUMI TACHI

These are prearranged sparring exercises that are intended to familiarise you with the applications of the *suburi* and the *awase* that you have been practising. They should be approached in the same manner as all aikido techniques: with full commitment, correct breathing and careful consideration for your partner. Care should be taken during the initial practices not to make contact as it is all too easy to forget what your next move should be and thus be caught by a swift partner when you hesitate.

Five *kumi tachi* are described here. However, it is important for you to realise that each of these five is subject to several variations as you progress. These are the basic forms of *kumi tachi* which you are expected to know during your early training in some styles. The term uke-tachi is used here to denote the person who is defending; uchi-tachi denotes your partner who is on the offensive during the practice. The descriptions will feature you (the reader) in the part of uke-tachi and your partner will be uchi-tachi.

First *Kumi Tachi* (Fig 72)

1. Both partners commence in *ken no kamae*, right posture with *bokken* tips crossed.
2. Raise your *bokken* as in the first *ken suburi*. Uchi-tachi will blend with your raise by entering forwards and to his left, performing a thrust and sideways cut (from his right to his left) at your chest level. Uchi-tachi finishes up with his feet side by side and his *bokken* protecting his head and pointing back towards your chest.
3. Step back with your left foot as uchi-

Figs 72(a–g)   First *kumi tachi*.

tachi enters, cutting with *shomen uchi* in right posture.
4. Uchi-tachi turns his *bokken* behind his head and enters in *hidari hanmi* to cut *shomen uchi* to your centre. Raise your *bokken* as for first *suburi*, stepping back with your right foot into *hidari hanmi*. Cut *shomen uchi* to your partner's centre, deflecting his cut to finish with your *bokken* pointing to his centre.
5. Uchi-tachi steps across to his right with his right foot, swinging his *bokken* up to protect his head as in fifth *suburi*. He adopts *migi hanmi* to perform right *shomen uchi* as you raise your *bokken* and step back with your left foot. Cut in *shomen uchi* to deflect uchi's cut and again finish with your *bokken* pointing directly to uchi-tachi's centre to conclude the encounter.

What actually occurs in this sequence is that you perform a series of cuts in first *suburi* while uchi tries to thrust and then perform two moves of the fifth suburi, both proving unsuccessful. Your deflections must be firm and your breathing controlled at all times. Take care not to make contact with your partner's thumbs and ensure that your cuts finish

Fig 72 (b)

Fig 72 (c)

Fig 72 (d)

Fig 72 (e)

Fig 72 (f)

Fig 72 (g)

Figs 73(a–l)   Second *kumi tachi*.

Fig 73 (b)

Fig 73 (e)

Fig 73 (f)

Fig 73 (i)

Fig 73 (j)

Fig 73 (c)

Fig 73 (d)

Fig 73 (g)

Fig 73 (h)

Fig 73 (k)

Fig 73 (l)

at the level of your partner's centre, rather than at his chest which is a common mistake.

Second *Kumi Tachi* (*Fig 73*)

1. Both partners commence in *ken no kamae*, right posture with *bokken* tips crossed.
2. Raise your *bokken* to perform first *suburi*. As you raise your weapon, uchi also raises his *bokken* to perform *shomen uchi komi* (second *suburi*). He steps forwards with his right foot and cuts to your right knee.
3. As uchi-tachi steps in, step back with your left foot, sliding your right foot back but remaining in right posture. Cut down against uchi's *bokken* with a defensive strike.
4. Now raise your *bokken* tip and begin to enter to make *kote* on uchi-tachi's left wrist. Uchi-tachi uses this opening to enter around your *bokken* in *hidari hanmi* and thrust to your centre.
5. Step back quickly into *hidari hanmi*, dropping the handle of your *bokken* in front of your centre to defend against uchi-tachi's thrust. Uchi-tachi steps across to his right into right posture, moving as in the fifth *suburi*, to cut in *shomen uchi*.
6. Step back with your left foot, raising your *bokken* and cutting *shomen uchi* to deflect uchi-tachi's *bokken* and finish with your *bokken* directed at his centre. Lay your *bokken* over uchi-tachi's *bokken* to deflect it downwards.
7. Uchi-tachi again uses this opening to enter around your *bokken* in left posture and thrust to your centre. Again, step back into left posture dropping the handle of your *bokken* in front of your centre in a defensive parry.
8. Uchi-tachi steps across to his right in

Figs 74(a–g)   Third *kumi tachi*.

fifth *suburi* and cuts in *shomen uchi*. Step back with your left foot and make *shomen uchi* to deflect uchi-tachi's cut and finish with your *bokken* pointing directly to uchi-tachi's centre to conclude the *kumi tachi*.

In this *kumi tachi* you have made two defensive parries while uchi has practised thrusting to an opening left by your defence.

Third *Kumi Tachi* (*Fig 74*)

1. Partners commence in *ken no kamae* with sword tips crossed. Lay your *bokken* firmly over uchi-tachi's to deflect it downwards and to your left as if it is your intention to thrust to his centre.
2. Uchi-tachi utilises this opening to enter around your *bokken* in left posture and thrust to your centre. Step back quickly into left posture, dropping the handle of your *bokken* in front of your centre to make a defensive parry.
3. Uchi-tachi now steps across to his right in fifth *suburi* to cut *shomen uchi* in right posture. As uchi-tachi raises his *bokken*, raise yours while stepping back with your left foot. Cut in *shomen uchi*,

Figs 74 (b)

Fig 74 (c)

Fig 74 (d)

Fig 74 (e)

Fig 74 (f)

Fig 74 (g)

deflecting uchi-tachi's *bokken* to finish with your *bokken* directed to uchi-tachi's centre.

This *kumi tachi* follows the lines of the previous one, except that it has concentrated attention to one portion of it where you are practising the basic parry and fifth *suburi* combination.

Fourth *Kumi Tachi* (*Fig 75*)

1.   Partners commence in *ken no kamae* as previously and uchi-tachi begins the exercise by thrusting in right posture to your centre.

2.   You must make your posture small without changing it (*hito e mi*) and hold uchi-tachi's *bokken* down as you align your *bokken* tip with uchi-tachi's centre. Uchi permits his *bokken* to flow around your *bokken* and steps forward in left posture to thrust to your centre again.

3.   Step back quickly into left posture, dropping the handle of your *bokken* to perform a defensive parry as in the previous *kumi tachi*. Uchi-tachi steps across

Figs 75(a–g)   Fourth *kumi tachi*.

Fig 75 (b)

Fig 75 (d)

Fig 75 (e)

100

to his right into *migi hanmi* performing the fifth *suburi* to cut in *shomen uchi*.

4. As uchi-tachi steps to his right, raise your *bokken*, stepping back with your left foot and cut *shomen uchi* to his centre, deflecting his *bokken*. Finish with your *bokken* pointing directly towards uchi-tachi's centre.

This *kumi tachi* utilises the technique of one *bokken* flowing around the other to enable the aggressor to perform his thrust. Again the fifth suburi is utilised by uchi-tachi whilst you defend successfully using the first suburi.

Fifth *Kumi Tachi* (*Fig 76*)

1. Partners commence as before in *ken no kamae*. Uchi-tachi raises his *bokken* to perform the second *suburi*, stepping back with his right foot and then forwards to cut in *shomen uchi komi*.

2. As uchi-tachi performs his cut, step to your left into left posture making fifth *suburi* and cutting *kote* to uchi-tachi's right wrist. Uchi steps forwards and to his left with his left foot into *hidari hanmi* to avoid your cut. He aligns his posture towards you and immediately steps back across into right posture making fifth *suburi* to cut *shomen uchi* to your centre.

3. Raise your *bokken* and step back into right posture, cutting *shomen uchi* to deflect uchi-tachi's *bokken* and finishing with your weapon pointing directly at uchi-tachi's centre. Now slide straight towards uchi-tachi with your right foot, pushing his *bokken* upwards to make an opening for you to control his weapon with your left hand as you

Fig 75 (c)

Fig 75 (f)

Fig 75 (g)

Figs 76(a–o)   Fifth *kumi tachi*.

Fig 76 (b)

Fig 76 (e)

Fig 76 (f)

Fig 76 (i)

Fig 76 (j)

Fig 76 (c)

Fig 76 (d)

Fig 76 (g)

Fig 76 (h)

Fig 76 (k)

Fig 76 (l)

Fig 76 (m)

Fig 76 (n)

Fig 76 (o)

step forwards again into uchi-tachi with your left foot.

4. Uchi-tachi spots an opening as his *bokken* is forced upwards to attack your exposed right leg. Uchi-tachi enters with his left foot, stepping around with his right to cut *gyaku yokomen* to your right leg. Seeing the cut coming, you pivot on your left foot, cutting down sharply in defence against uchi-tachi's cut.

5. Uchi-tachi steps across to his right, making fifth *suburi* to cut *shomen uchi* to your centre. Raise your *bokken*, step back with your left foot to cut *shomen uchi* to uchi-tachi's centre, deflecting his *bokken* and concluding with your *bokken* pointing directly to uchi-tachi's centre.

In this *kumi tachi* you take some of the initiative by attempting to control uchi's-tachi *bokken* with your left hand. Uchi-tachi sees this coming and forces you into a defensive position by cutting to your leg. The finish is, however, similar to the previous *kumi tachi*.

TACHI DORI

Tachi dori roughly translated means 'sword-taking', and several exercises are practised to disarm the holder of his sword and subdue him. Many of these techniques are combined with the immobilisation and projection techniques, and are not usually taught until you reach a senior level within your club. Certainly, a fair amount of experience is required before you practice these techniques regularly. Others, however, may be combined with *kokyu nage*, and these are simpler for the beginner to perform.

To practise *tachi dori* you must first become familiar with the entry when faced with an adversary using a *bokken* or sword. It can be extremely unnerving to come face to face with a live blade, so all initial practice is carried out using the *bokken*. Even the *bokken* can prove to be quite intimidating, so you will require a great deal of practise with your partner in these basic exercises.

Preliminary Practice (*Fig 77*)

Face one another in *migi hanmi*, your partner holding his *bokken* in *ken no kamae*. Your partner will perform the first *suburi* in such a manner that, if you do not move, you will be struck on the centre of your head. Obviously, it is prudent to commence practice slowly and to build up speed very gradually.

As your partner commences his cut, and not before, step to your right and forwards with your right foot, bringing your left foot around into right posture. This posture will bring you round to face your partner as he finishes his cut, your body having moved off the line of the cut. This movement is essentially the same as you performed for the first *awase* (partner practice), except that you do not hold your *bokken*.

You can perform this to either side of the *bokken*, depending upon which *hanmi* you are in at the time. The entry to uchi-tachi's right side is shown in Fig 77 and, in this case, a defensive blending action is being demonstrated combined with *atemi* to uchi-tachi's face.

Implicit in this exercise is a promised attack by your partner. He will cut to where you were standing and will not follow your movement as you evade his blade. To give credibility to the attack you must make your move at the last possible moment.

Atemi performed during this exercise will provide you with the feeling of correct distancing.

First *Tachi Dori* (*Fig 78*)

Commence by facing one another in right posture, your partner holding his *bokken* in *ken no kamae*. Your partner commences by making the first *suburi*, stepping forwards to cut to your centre. As his *bokken* descends, step into right posture to evade the *bokken* as it cuts downwards. In this case, your posture should be at a wide angle, about 90 degrees to uke.

Step in close to uke putting your right hand over the handle of his *bokken* and between his hands. Raise the *bokken* to just above your head height, stepping to your right front to cut the *bokken* down towards uke's third point. This will unbalance uke as you bring your right arm down in a sweeping motion, exhaling as you do this. Your partner will roll away in *ukemi*, releasing the *bokken* rather than risking getting bruised by it as you are now controlling the weapon.

Fig 77   Preliminary practice for *tachi dori*.

Figs 78(a–d)   First *Tachi dori*.

Fig 78 (b)

Fig 78 (c)

Fig 78 (d)

Second *Tachi Dori* (Fig 79)

Commence in right posture with your partner holding his *bokken* in *ken no kamae*. Your partner begins by making second *suburi*, stepping forwards to cut to your centre. As his *bokken* descends,

step to your left and forwards with your left foot to enter with a *tenkai* motion (*see* Glossary), finishing in right posture beside and slightly in front of uke. With your left hand grasp the *bokken* from above between uke's hands and bring your right hand to the back of the blade.

106

Figs 79(a–c)   Second *Tachi dori*.

Fig 79 (b)

Fig 79 (c)

Holding the *bokken* handle with your left hand, lift it as you push the blade down and inwards towards your partner, at the same time turning your posture towards him. Step round and back with your left foot, drawing uke forwards while pushing the blade up towards him to perform a sweeping upwards cut through his centre.

Third *Tachi Dori* (Fig 80)

Commence in right posture with your partner holding his *bokken* in *ken no kamae*. Your partner commences by

Figs 80(a–e)   Third *Tachi dori*.

making the second *suburi*, cutting to your centre. Make entry forwards and to your left with your left foot, in the same manner as the previous *tachi dori*, to finish beside uke in right posture to match him.

Reach across with your right hand to

Fig 80 (b)

Fig 80 (c)

Fig 80 (d)

Fig 80 (e)

grasp the handle of his *bokken* between his hands. Bring your left arm up under uke's chin while sliding your left foot across behind him as in the *kokyu ho* exercise described in Chapter 3. Raise the *bokken* and turn your body to your left, retaining hold of the *bokken* as uke makes backward *ukemi* away from you across the mat.

These three *tachi dori* exercises conclude this chapter on the use of the sword in aikido. The techniques described are not exhaustive: there are many more to learn later as well as variations on those outlined here. A thorough knowledge of these techniques should provide you with a sound grounding upon which to extend your training in this area.

7   *Aiki Jo* – The Wooden Stave

In inaugurating aikido, the Founder did not identify it with a mere consolidation of . . . martial arts. He created aikido by compounding the merits of ancient arts with the 'Principle of Aiki' and incorporating into it all the elements common to every martial art.

Morihiro Saito (1975)

The *jo* is a stout wooden stave fashioned from Japanese oak which was originally used as a substitute for the long sword and the short spear. Its use in aikido has developed along various lines and it is now commonly in use as a separate entity around which many exercises, techniques and *kata* are based.

The principal use for the *jo* is as a weapon to counter and attack other aggressors who are armed with similar weapons, as a weapon to be neutralised or to neutralise an unarmed attacker, and as a visible extension of your personality. Use of the *jo* is also a very good method of achieving co-ordination of body, limbs and mind and, to this end, many exercises have been developed using it.

The teaching of *jo waza* (*jo* technique) may be broken down into separate sections. The initial section must deal with the fundamental movements required to use the weapon and these, as with the *bokken*, are termed *suburi*. There are twenty *jo suburi* in total, which demonstrates the versatility of this weapon as opposed to the sword, for which there are only seven *suburi* as taught in aikido.

The next section contains the 31 count *kata*, (prearranged sequences of individual exercises) in the use of the *jo* against imaginary opponents armed with similar weapons. At advanced levels, the *kata* may be demonstrated using a partner who will go through a similar, pre-arranged set of moves designed to blend with and complement the *kata*.

Finally, the third section will contain detailed descriptions of some of the various partner exercises which are termed *kumi jo*. Basic exercises in extension and disarming will be included in the chapter on advanced techniques. There is a great deal of knowledge required to achieve a satisfactory level of expertise with the *jo* and in learning you will tend to pick up useful experience in body co-ordination and posture along the way.

JO SUBURI

Each of the following twenty *suburi* should be practised carefully and with feeling. Breathing is very important and you should inhale before you start the

Figs 81(a–d)   *Choku tsuki*: first *jo suburi*.

Fig 81 (b)

Fig 81 (c)

Fig 81 (d)

movements, allowing your breath to pass out of your lungs as you perform the *suburi*, and exhaling sharply as you finish the final thrust or strike of the *suburi*. Always check your posture at the beginning and end of each *suburi* to ensure that you have started and finished correctly. Good posture before and after performance goes a long way towards correct posture during the *suburi*.

First *Jo Suburi* – *Choku Tsuki* (*Fig 81*)

This is the basic thrusting movement which is featured in many of the *jo waza*. Commence in basic posture, *hidari hanmi*, with the *jo* resting on one end vertically on the mat immediately in front of your left foot. Hold the *jo* with your left hand (as shown in Fig 81a).

Figs 82(a–c)   *Kaeshi tsuki: second jo suburi.*

Reach down with your right hand to grasp the *jo* near its base. Your left hand should lift the *jo* as you do this. Slide your right hand down to the end as you bring the *jo* to a horizontal position, *tsuki no kamae*. Slide the *jo* through your left hand back and then forwards, swinging your right hand up to the front of your centre. Both feet slide forwards as you lower your posture during this forward thrust.

Second *Jo Suburi – Kaeshi Tsuki* (Fig 82)

This is actually a counter to a thrust from your opponent. Commence in left posture as for the first *jo suburi*. Grasp the top of the *jo* with your right hand, thumb downwards. Bring the *jo* up in a circular motion as you move to your left with your left foot, bringing your right foot around to remain in *hidari hanmi*. As you move, thrust the *jo* forwards to your opponent's centre, your left hand on top of the *jo*. Expel your breath explosively as the thrust is performed.

Fig 82 (b)

Fig 82 (c)

Figs 83(a–d)   *Ushiro tsuki*: third *jo suburi*.

Fig 83 (b)

Fig 83 (c)

Fig 83 (d)

Third *Jo Suburi – Ushiro Tsuki* (Fig 83)

This is a thrust against an opponent who is behind you. Commence in basic posture as for the previous *suburi* (*kaeshi tsuki*), bringing your right hand to the top of the *jo*, thumb upwards. Lift the *jo*, placing it along the underside of your left forearm while sliding your left foot back beside your right. Step back with your left foot, thrusting the *jo* straight to your rear and turning your body to your left as you do this.

Figs 84(a–c)   *Tsuki gedan gaeshi:* fourth *jo suburi.*

Fig 84 (b)

Fig 84 (c)

Fourth *Jo Suburi – Tsuki Gedan Gaeshi* (*Fig 84*)

This is the first of two combinations of movements which incorporate the first *suburi*. This combination can be practised as a routine with a partner.

Commence in *hidari tsuki no kamae* (*see* Glossary), holding the *jo* horizontally in your left hand with your right hand at its base, your feet in left posture. Swing back with your right hand to make *choku tsuki* (first *jo suburi*), sliding your feet forwards. Slide your left hand towards the front of the *jo* and step backwards and to the right, remaining in left posture as you push the *jo* back past your right side through your right hand.

Turn your hips to the left, stepping forwards with your right foot, and bringing the *jo* round at knee level to strike at your opponent's lower legs. Your right hand should be behind the *jo* pushing it round to make contact.

Fifth *Jo Suburi – Tsuki Jodan Gaeshi* (*Fig 85*)

This combination introduces the striking techniques which are to follow in the next five *suburi*. You commence in *hidari tsuki no kamae* (as in the previous *suburi*). Swing back with your right hand to perform *choku tsuki*, sliding your feet forwards. Move backwards and to the right, still in *hidari hanmi*, bringing the *jo* up to protect your head (basic block). Turn it over your head to the striking position in preparation for *shomen uchi* strike.

The strike is identical to *shomen uchi* with the *bokken*, and is performed as you step forwards with your right foot, bringing the *jo* straight down to your opponent's centre.

Figs 85(a–d)   *Tsuki jodan gaeshi*: fifth *jo suburi*.

Fig 85 (b)

Fig 85 (c)

Fig 85 (d)

Sixth *Jo Suburi – Shomen Uchi Komi* (Fig 86)

This striking movement follows the pattern of the second *ken suburi* (*see* page 80), as its title implies. Commence in right posture holding the *jo* as you would the *bokken*. Step back with your right foot, raising the *jo* above your head, pointing it towards the ceiling and angled back slightly.

As you step forwards with your right

115

Figs 86(a–c)   *Shomen uchi komi*: sixth *jo suburi*.

foot, bring your hands down and forwards, striking with the *jo* to your opponent's centre.

Seventh *Jo Suburi – Renzoku Uchi Komi* (Fig 87)

This *suburi* is very similar to the fifth *ken suburi* (*see* page 84).

Commence in right posture holding the *jo* as you would a *bokken* and perform *shomen uchi komi* as described in the sixth *jo suburi*.

Having performed the strike in right posture, move your weight forwards on to your right foot and bring your hands up to the front of, and just above, your head with the *jo* pointing to your right.

Step forwards with your left foot, turning your hips into left posture. Bring the *jo* round to extend behind you and make *hidari shomen uchi* to complete the *suburi*.

Fig 86 (b)

Fig 86 (c)

Fig 87 (b)

Figs 87(a–e)   *Renzoku uchi komi*: seventh *jo suburi*.

Fig 87 (c)

Fig 87 (d)

Fig 87 (e)

Fig 88 (b)

Figs 88(a–e)   *Men uchi gedan gaeshi*: eighth *jo suburi.*

Fig 88 (c)

Fig 88 (d)

Fig 88 (e)

Fig 89 (b)

Fig 89 (c)

Fig 89 (d)

Figs 89(a–d)   *Men uchi ushiro tsuki*: ninth *jo suburi*.

Eighth *Jo Suburi* – *Men Uchi Gedan Gaeshi* (Fig 88)

This combination move incorporates a striking routine similar to the fourth *jo suburi*. Commence in right posture. Hold the *jo* as you would a *bokken* and perform *shomen uchi komi* (sixth *jo suburi*). When the strike is completed, extend your right hand to the end of the *jo*, sweep it back to your left side and move back and to your left.

Step forwards with your left foot. Bring the *jo* round in a strike to your opponent's knee, keeping your left hand behind the *jo* to give power to the strike.

Ninth *Jo Suburi* – *Men Uchi Ushiro Tsuki* (Fig 89)

This is a combination of the sixth and third *jo suburi*. Commence in right posture to perform *shomen uchi komi* (sixth

Figs 90(a–e) *Gyaku yokomen ushiro tsuki*:
tenth *jo suburi*.

Fig 90 (b)

Fig 90 (c)

Fig 90 (d)

jo suburi). As the strike is completed, slide your right hand to the forward end of the *jo*, turn your hips into left posture and perform a thrust to the rear at chest level as in *ushiro tsuki*.

Tenth *Jo Suburi – Gyaku Yokomen Ushiro Tsuki* (*Fig 90*)

Similar to the previous *suburi*, this incorporates elements of the seventh and third *jo suburi*. Commence in right posture as if you had just completed *shomen uchi komi* (sixth *jo suburi*), bringing your hands up to the front of, and just above, your head, the *jo* pointing to your right. Step forwards with your left foot and perform *hidari shomen uchi*.

Slide your left hand to the front end of the *jo*, turning your hips further into left posture and perform *ushiro tsuki* to your right side at chest level.

Figs 91(a–e) *Katate gedan gaeshi*: eleventh *jo suburi*.

Fig 90 (e)

Fig 91 (b)

121

Fig 91 (c)

Fig 91 (d)

Fig 91 (e)

Eleventh *Jo Suburi – Katate Gedan Gaeshi* (Fig 91)

This is the first of the *suburi* which features one-hand grip and uses wrist movement for successful completion. Commence in *hidari tsuki no kamae*, sliding your left hand to the forward end of the *jo*. Push the *jo* back through your right hand, bringing your body back and to the right, as in the fourth *suburi*. Both hands should now be at the forward end of the *jo*.

Take a long step forwards with your right foot, sweeping the *jo* forwards across an imaginary opponent's face, holding it with your right hand only and catching it with your left hand over your head on your left side after the sweep is complete, finishing in a defensive position.

Twelfth *Jo Suburi – Toma Katate Uchi* (Fig 92)

This movement is used to extend the *jo* forwards to reach a considerable distance past your normal fighting range. Commence in *hidari tsuki no kamae* and draw the *jo* back over your head to your left with your right hand, resting the forward end of the *jo* on your left thumb/forefinger cleft. Draw your weight back on to your right foot.

As you start to swing the *jo* around with your right wrist, commence stepping forwards with your right foot, swinging the *jo* at your opponent's head and around to be caught by your left hand down by your left hip.

Thirteenth *Jo Suburi – Katate Hachi-No-Ji-Gaeshi* (Fig 93)

This incorporates a double wrist action to loosen your wrist and serves as the

Figs 92(a–e) *Toma katate uchi*: twelfth *jo suburi*.

Fig 92 (b)

Fig 92 (c)

Fig 92 (d)

Fig 92 (e)

Figs 93(a–g)   *Kata hachi-no-ji-gaeshi*:
thirteenth *jo suburi*.

Fig 93 (b)

Fig 93 (e)

Fig 93 (f)

Fig 93 (c)

Fig 93 (d)

Fig 93 (g)

precursor to the *hasso* techniques that will follow. Commence in left posture. Hold the *jo* in your right hand on your right side, the end resting on the mat. Turn your wrist forwards, raising the *jo* and, while stepping forwards with the right foot, sweep the *jo* across your imaginary opponent's face. Catch the *jo* high on your left side in your open left hand.

Swing your hips back to your right, changing posture into *hidari hanmi* while stepping back with your right foot as you push the *jo* across to your right with your left hand. Spin it around your right wrist, catching the short end in your left hand, beside your head on your right side.

Fourteenth *Jo Suburi – Hasso Gaeshi Uchi* (Fig 94)

The next five *suburi* all incorporate the *hasso* technique which consists of

Figs 94(a–f)   *Hasso gaeshi uchi*: fourteenth *jo suburi*.

Fig 94 (b)

Fig 94 (c)

Fig 94 (d)

Fig 94 (e)

Fig 94 (f)

rapidly twirling the *jo* from a forward position under your wrist and up to above your right shoulder beside your head, as you do to complete the thirteenth *suburi*.

Commence in *ken no kamae*, sliding your right foot back as you extend your left hand forwards and upwards, letting your right hand slide a little further towards the centre of the *jo*. As you step back with your right foot, push sharply down with your left had on the *jo* to swing it down and up to your rear. Grasp the bottom end with your left hand as it comes to a vertical position at the right side of your head in *hasso no kamae* (*see* Glossary).

Start to step forwards with your right foot as you bring the *jo* up to your head, changing the grip with your right hand, and complete your step forwards as you strike with *shomen uchi* in right posture.

Fifteenth *Jo Suburi – Hasso Gaeshi Tsuki* (Fig 95)

Commence as in the previous *suburi* from *ken no kamae*, twirling the *jo* to assume *hasso no kamae*. From this point, extend your left foot forwards, bringing the *jo* down to perform a straight thrust to your front. Slide your right hand forwards and perform *hasso gaeshi* once more, bringing your left foot back a little to finish in *hasso no kamae*.

Figs 95(a–e) *Hasso gaeshi tsuki*: fifteenth *jo suburi*, from *hasso no kamae*.

Fig 95 (b)

Fig 95 (c)

Fig 95 (d)

Fig 95 (e)

Figs 96(a–c)   *Hasso gaeshi ushiro tsuki*:
sixteenth *jo suburi*, from *hasso no kamae*.

Fig 96 (b)

Fig 96 (c)

Sixteenth *Jo Suburi* – *Hasso Gaeshi Ushiro Tsuki* (Fig 96)

Commence as in the previous *suburi* by twirling your *jo* to assume *hasso no kamae*. From the vertical, drop the top of the *jo* forwards, extending your left hand to its front end and thrusting the *jo* to your right rear (*migi ushiro tsuki*). Finish with your hips facing to your right.

Figs 97(a–c)   *Hasso gaeshi ushiro uchi:*
seventeenth *jo suburi*, from *hasso no kamae*.

Fig 97 (b)

Fig 97 (c)

Figs 98(a–c)   *Hasso gaeshi ushiro harai:*
eighteenth *jo suburi*, from *hasso no kamae*.

Seventeenth *Jo Suburi – Hasso Gaeshi Ushiro Uchi* (Fig 97)

Commence as in the sixteenth *suburi*, assuming *hasso no kamae*. Turn your hips further to your right and strike down and around to your rear with a round sweeping blow, keeping your feet in the same position as they were in *hasso no kamae*.

Eighteenth *Jo Suburi – Hasso Gaeshi Ushiro Harai* (Fig 98)

Commence as in the previous *suburi* to assume *hasso no kamae*. Turn your whole body to your rear, sweeping your right foot back and round whilst swinging the *jo* in a sweeping strike to an imaginary opponent who is standing behind you.

Fig 98 (b)

Fig 98 (c)

Nineteenth *Jo Suburi – Hidari Nagare Gaeshi Uchi* (Fig 99)

These final two suburi are designed to help improve your body movement as they incorporate a flowing combination of strikes. Commence in *ken no kamae* (right posture), stepping back with your right foot to perform *shomen uchi komi* (sixth *jo suburi*). As the strike is made, turn to your left, bringing the *jo* around as you extend your left hand forwards to catch it.

From here, take the *jo* back over your head. You should now be facing your rear as you perform right *shomen uchi* strike to the imaginary opponent who is now standing in front of you.

Figs 99(a–e) *Hidari nagare gaeshi uchi*: nineteenth *jo suburi*.

Fig 99 (b)

Fig 99 (c)

Fig 99 (d)

Fig 99 (e)

Figs 100(a–h) *Migi nagare gaeshi tsuki*: twentieth *jo suburi*.

Fig 100 (b)

Fig 100 (c)

Fig 100 (d)

Fig 100 (e)

Fig 100 (f)

Fig 100 (g)

Fig 100 (h)

Twentieth *Jo Suburi – Migi Nagare Gaeshi Tsuki* (*Fig 100*)

Commence in *ken no kamae* (right posture), stepping forwards with your left foot to perform *hidari shomen uchi*. As you complete the strike, step back and round with your right foot, turning to your rear to block across your head. Lower your hands into *hidari tsuki no kamae* and perform *hidari choku tsuki* (first *jo suburi*) to deal with the imaginary adversary behind you.

JO KATA

There are two main *kata* which include the majority of the *suburi* within their performance. As there are no specific names for·these *kata* they are classified according to the number of separate movements contained within them.

The 13 count *kata* is a short pattern which includes striking and thrusting combined with basic blocks and a *hasso no kamae* movement at the half-way point. The 31 count *kata* is a longer pattern which may be practised as a partner exercise between two experienced aikidoka. As with most *kata* you should aim to complete on the spot where you started.

The 31 count *kata* is the most important of the two and is the main one required during gradings. Any of the *kata* must be performed with total commitment, each move being directed against an imaginary opponent who is attacking you. Every strike, thrust or block should be completed meaningfully. The final thrust or strike of the *kata* represents the fatal blow, and should be accompanied with a forceful expulsion of breath.

Aiki Jo No Sanjuichi No Kata – 31 Count Kata (*Fig 101*)

The moves of the 31 Count Kata are illustrated on pages 135–143, and should be viewed from left to right.

Commence in basic posture *hidari hanmi*, holding the *jo* vertically in your left hand, one end resting on the mat in front of your left foot.

1. Slide forwards and to your left with both feet in left posture, grasping the top of the *jo* with your right hand, thumb down, and make *kaeshi tsuki* (second *jo suburi*) to your imaginary opponent.
2. Move back and to your right, bringing the *jo* up by raising your right hand over your head to make a defensive block.
3. Bring the *jo* down again and step forwards and to the left to perform *choku tsuki* in left posture.
4. Slide back to your right (as in the second move) raising the *jo* overhead, with both hands at the centre of the *jo*.
5. Step forwards with your right foot into right posture to make *shomen uchi* strike.
6. Raise your *jo* and step forwards with your left foot to make *hidari shomen uchi* strike.
7. Turn to your right through 180 degrees, bringing the *jo* back over your head and step forwards with your right foot to perform *migi shomen uchi* strike.
8. Step forwards with your left foot, raising the *jo* as in the fifth *jo suburi*, to perform *hidari shomen uchi* strike.
9. Bring your right foot back around as you turn to your right through 180 degrees, sweeping the *jo* around in *ushiro harai* (see Glossary).
10. From *ushiro harai* step to your left and bring your right foot up beside your left, sweeping the *jo* in an upward strike while bringing your hands in front of and just above your head. The *jo* stops, pointing to your right front.
11. Raise your hands and turn the *jo* behind your head, striking *hidari shomen uchi* as you step forwards with your left foot.
12. Bring your weight back so that it is distributed evenly between your feet and lower the *jo* to adopt *tsuki no kamae*.
13. Slide both feet forwards to perform *choku tsuki*.
14. Step back and to your right with your right foot while making a basic defensive block.
15. Swing the *jo* around behind you, stepping forwards with your right foot to perform *shomen uchi*.
16. Extend your right hand to the front of the *jo*, pulling your weight back on to your left foot as you slide the *jo* back to the left side of your body (as in the eighth *jo suburi*).
17. Step forwards with your left foot, swinging your hips round to your right and sweeping the *jo* round to strike to your opponent's knee.
18. Step back and to your right, turning the *jo* end over end to assume *tsuki no kamae* in left posture.
19. Perform *choku tsuki* to your opponent's knee.
20. Raise the *jo* in a basic block, continuing the movement to sweep it round to the back of your head to make *shomen uchi* as you step forwards with your right foot.
21. Drop your weight back, sinking on to your left knee to slide the *jo* back along the left side of your body with your right hand.
22. Rise from the floor bringing the *jo* up, and step forwards with your left foot to thrust forwards at chest height with the lower end of the *jo*.
23. Move backwards and to the right, turning the *jo* end over end by sliding your right hand forwards in front of your left hand, and then pulling the *jo* over to strike at your opponent's *jo* from above.
24. Stepping forwards in left posture, perform *choku tsuki*.
25. Step forwards again in left posture to make a second *choku tsuki*.

140

26. Slide your left hand forwards and draw the *jo* back to the right side of your body while remaining in left posture.

27. Withdraw your left foot to the rear, adopting right posture, while sweeping the *jo* around to defend against your opponent's strike to your knee.

28. Bring the *jo* up to your left side and make a straight thrust to your opponent's eyes.

29. Turn the *jo* over and lower it to your left side, remaining in right posture in preparation for *choku tsuki*.

30. Step forwards with your right foot and perform *choku tsuki*.

31. Bring the *jo* around your right side to make *shomen uchi* as you step forwards and to your left with your left foot, sliding your right foot into *hidari hanmi*. Your *jo* should almost make contact with your partner's head (if you are practising this with a partner) as you complete the *kata* with an explosive exhalation of breath.

KUMI JO

After practising the *suburi* and the *kata*, your instructor will guide you on to performing various exercises to enable you to practise blending and to obtain experience of working with a partner. (The exercises will vary with each instructor and it is not possible to include all the variations within this text.)

The purpose of these exercises is to prepare you for the main set partner practices which are called *kumi jo*. There are ten basic exercises in *kumi jo*, but only the first three are described here. Their purpose is to ensure that you gain experience in the use of your *jo* against an opponent and, most importantly, to develop the sense of fighting distance necessary to keep yourself from getting hurt too often.

Like the *suburi* and the *kata*, these exercises must be practised with spirit and total commitment: they are not purely mechanical movements to be performed with detachment – you will only get out of them what you put in. Naturally, you must exert full control over your *jo* so that if your partner, who is substituting for an opponent, makes a mistake, you do not carry the technique through to the finish. Without control, you may soon run short of willing partners.

First *Kumi Jo* (Fig 102)

1. Commence in basic posture, *hidari hanmi*, holding your *jo* vertically in front of your left foot with your left hand.
2. Uke commences in *tsuki no kamae*, left posture, holding the *jo* at the ready. Uke begins by making *choku tsuki* to your chest.
3. Step to your left with your left foot to bring your body out of the line of uke's thrust, your right foot following so that you remain in left posture facing uke. Your right hand grasps the top of the *jo*, thumb downwards, and you perform *kaeshi tsuki* to uke's chest.
4. Uke brings his right foot around to his rear left to face you in left posture, making a spiral deflection to knock your *jo* off line. He now performs *choku tsuki* to your chest again.
5. Step back and to your right with your right foot, bringing your left foot across into left posture. As you do this, bring your *jo* up in a basic overhead block to deflect uke's thrust upwards.
6. Turn your *jo* over your head, stepping forwards with your right foot to make *shomen uchi komi* to uke's head,
7. Uke steps back with his left foot, bringing the rear end of his *jo* up to deflect your strike. Uke steps forwards with his right foot to perform a thrust to your eyes.
8. Step forwards and to your left to avoid uke's thrust, making *shomen uchi komi* in left posture to uke's head.

Second *Kumi Jo* (Fig 103)

1. Commence in basic posture, as in the first *kumi jo*.
2. Uke commences in *hidari hanmi tsuki no kamae*. Uke makes *choku tsuki* towards your chest.

Figs 102(a–j)   First *kumi jo*.

Fig 102 (b)

Fig 102 (c)

Fig 102 (d)

Fig 102 (e)

Fig 102 (f)

Fig 102 (g)

Fig 102 (h)

Fig 102 (i)

Fig 102 (j)

Figs 103(a–e)   Second *kumi jo*.

Fig 103 (b)

Fig 103 (c)

Fig 103 (d)

3.   Lift your *jo* in a circular movement, deflecting uke's *jo* with the top of yours. Catch hold of your *jo* at the bottom with your right hand as you do this. Step to your left with your right foot behind you, then enter with your left foot and make *choku tsuki* towards uke's chest.

4.   Uke steps forwards and to his right with his right foot entering around your thrust to strike *migi yokomen uchi komi* to your left knee.

5.   Move to your right in left posture, making a defensive block to stop uke's strike.

6.   Uke now makes *choku tsuki* towards your exposed right side.

7.   Step to your left in left posture to avoid uke's thrust and finish the set with *choku tsuki* to uke's right side.

Fig 103 (e)

Third *Kumi Jo* (Fig 104)

1.   Commence in basic posture as in the second *kumi jo*.

2.   Uke commences in *hidari hanmi tsuki no kamae*. He makes *choku tsuki* towards your knees.

3.   Step to your left with your right foot behind you, lifting your *jo* in a circular

movement to block uke's *jo* with the bottom of your *jo*.

4.   Uke makes *choku tsuki* towards your exposed left side.

5.   Step to your right into left posture, turning the *jo* end over end and striking uke's *jo* down and away. Turn towards uke and make *choku tsuki* towards his chest.

6.   Uke attempts to deflect your *jo* by pulling his *jo* across to his left in a semi-circular motion.

7.   Blend with uke's defence and, with a spiral movement, perform a second *choku tsuki* over the top of uke's *jo* to his centre.

147

Figs 104(a–g)   Third *kumi jo*.

Fig 104 (b)

Fig 104 (c)

Fig 104 (d)

Fig 104 (e)

Fig 104 (f)

Fig 104 (g)

These first three *kumi jo* exercises will help you to develop timing and co-ordination as well as giving you the feel of working with a partner. As you progress, you will be shown further exercises in this series which involve the use of more difficult *jo suburi* and *tai sabkai* (body movement). Practice with the *jo* can be great fun as long as you approach it with care and thought for your partner. Enjoy your practice and you will eventually begin to feel the benefits. In his book, *Dynamic Aikido*, Gozo Shioda states:

'... aikido is more than simply a physical skill. To co-ordinate with the opponent's movement and power it is necessary that the mind as well as the body be pliant. In other words the mind must be alert and flexible in order to take advantage of the opponent's movements. Taken a step further, this means that the aikidoka must understand his opponent and share his feelings; so the final objective is not to inflict injury but to cultivate a sense of harmony.'

8 *Kokyu Nage* – The Spirit of Aikido

... true aikido is not merely having a strong body, it is not simply muscular strength. It is the unification of the mind and body. If a spirit which remains unperturbed whatever the crisis, whatever the circumstances is not cultivated, then a person cannot be called strong as a man.

Kisshomaru Ueshiba (1978)

The practice of *kokyu nage* is the closest that we come to touching the true spirit of aikido. For *kokyu nage* to be performed well, it is essential to achieve

Fig 105   *Aiki Otoshi.*

unification of mind and body, to blend with your partner and to breathe correctly and without haste. The spirit should remain at ease during *kokyu nage* and your whole person should be calm and composed during the practice. This is the message that is being imparted in this chapter, and the words of O Sensei's son, Kisshomaru Ueshiba, illustrate this theme as it applies to aikido generally. I have extracted his words and used them in the context of *kokyu nage*, as I feel that they apply to this section of your training probably more than to any other.

Kokyu nage, well performed, looks extremely simple. However, when you attempt it initially, you will soon realise that it is by no means easy at all. You must first learn to blend, and then to follow. Following alone is difficult until you have practised it at length, and even well-seasoned aikidoka can experience difficulties with following at times. The exercises for blending described in Chapter 3 will lead you into the practice of *kokyu nage*. The proper control of your breathing is vital to the correct execution of each technique, and will make the difference between empty and live technique.

In preparation for *kokyu nage*, all aikidoka must learn to follow their partners, and exercises in following will be practised at various times during club sessions. Tori (the person performing the technique) will lead uke's hand in circular movements, up and down, until uke finds that he becomes obliged to perform *ukemi*. Such leading/following exercises may appear to have little relationship to real technique, but it is important for you to master them if you are to avoid injury during the practice of more advanced techniques. You will find that *ukemi* becomes easier if you are conversant with the concept of following.

The initial exercises in *kokyu nage* involve the extension of *tai no henko* into a projection, as described in Chapter 3. This includes the blending into *tai no henko* from a fluid position (*ki no nagare*) and the act of leading your partner forwards and around you into *ukemi*. *Kokyu nage* may be practised in pairs, taking turns to be uke, or in line-ups of several students, one performing the technique while the others act as ukes. Once some measure of proficiency has been attained, it may be practised with all students in a large circle around *tori* who offers one or both of his hands to each in turn and will throw with various *kokyu nage* techniques.

The exercises described here in detail are intended to introduce the beginner to the principles of leading and blending. The development of *kokyu nage* will occur at a much later stage once you are thoroughly familiar with the required movements. *Kokyu nage* is a free and flexible form of practice which defies

detailed description, occurring spontaneously as a reaction to whatever attack you are subject to from your partner.

Ai Hanmi Katate Dori (*Fig 106*)

Perform this from *ki no nagare* as your partner steps towards you to grasp your right (or left) wrist with his right (or left) hand. This may be likened to a flexible first form (*see Fig 13*, page 32) where your partner is moving towards you with the intention of pushing you backwards as he holds your wrist.

As uke grasps your right wrist, swivel to your left through 180 degrees, leading uke past you. You will now have adopted left posture, having blended with uke's forward motion. Raise your right arm as you commence stepping forwards with your right foot. Complete the technique by exhaling as you step forwards into right posture, extending your right arm forwards and downwards, turning your handblades outwards to augment your power. This will project uke forwards across the mat into *ukemi*.

Irimi Tenkan Form (*Fig 107*)

As uke steps forwards to grasp your right wrist with his right hand, enter with your left foot towards uke's right side while turning through 180 degrees around to your right. Step round with your right foot to arrive in left posture, facing in the same direction as uke's attack. Uke will be carried around your body by your turning motion so that he will finish beside you, still grasping your right wrist and facing in the same direction as you. Step out to your left with

Figs 106(a–d)   Basic *kokyu nage* from *ai hanmi katate dori*.

Fig 106 (c)

Figs 106 (b)

Fig 106 (d)

Figs 107(a–f)   *Irimi tenkan kokyu nage* from *ai hanmi katate dori*.

Fig 107 (b)

Fig 107 (c)

Fig 107 (d)

Fig 107 (e)

Fig 107 (f)

Figs 108(a–f)   *Tenkan kokyu nage* from *ai hanmi katate dori*.

Fig 108 (b)

Fig 108 (c)

Fig 108 (d)

Fig 108 (e)

Fig 108 (f)

155

your left foot, then forwards with your right foot, exhaling as you extend your right arm forwards and downwards to project uke across the mat into *ukemi.*

Tenkan Form *(Fig 108)*

As uke steps forwards to grasp your right wrist with his right hand, turn away from him by stepping back and around with your left foot through 180 degrees, drawing uke around you as you turn. As you complete your turn, lower your right arm and reverse its direction of travel as you begin to turn back slightly to your right, taking a small step to your right with your right foot.

Uke will follow your movement so that his right arm finishes across your body. Bring your left arm up and forwards, palm of the hand upwards, under uke's right armpit, and as you step forwards with your left foot, extend both your arms forwards, turning your hands inwards as you exhale. Your left arm will help to project uke across the mat into *ukemi.*

Other Forms

You may perform *kokyu nage* from *ai hanmi katate dori* in several ways, gen-erally by leading uke either downwards to the mat or up and over backwards. If you turn inwards – to your right – when uke is grasping your right wrist, you may lead him in a downward spiral around your body to culminate in *ukemi.*

If you wish, you may lead uke down-wards initially, then in a wide sweeping arc upwards, directing his power back on to him to force him to perform back-ward *ukemi* on to the mat. For a demon-stration of this principle, see page 160, *ryote dori* (two-handed attack).

Gyaku Hanmi Katate Dori *(Fig 109)*

Uke steps towards you to grasp your right wrist with his left hand. As he does this, turn as in *tai no henko*, drawing uke's grip forwards in the direction of his travel. Step forwards with your right foot, raising your right arm forwards and extending it downwards as you exhale to help project uke across the mat. This is essentially the same move-ment as you practised earlier when you extended *tai no henko* into *kokyu nage.*

From this basic technique, you may perform several variations including leading uke around you either way in a

Fig 109 (a–b) *Kokyu nage* from *gyaku hanmi katate dori*, basic form.

Fig 109 (b)

Fig 110 (a–b)   *Kokyu nage* from *gyaku hanmi katate dori, irimi* form.

Fig 110 (b)

Fig 111 (a–c)   *Ryote dori kokyu nage*, basic form.

Fig 111 (b)

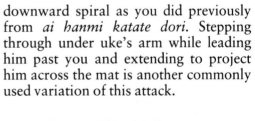

downward spiral as you did previously from *ai hanmi katate dori*. Stepping through under uke's arm while leading him past you and extending to project him across the mat is another commonly used variation of this attack.

Irimi Form (*Fig 110*)

As uke steps forward to grasp your left wrist with his right hand, step forwards and to your left with your left foot, applying *atemi* to uke's face with your right fist to break his posture and concentration.

Fig 111 (c)

Insert your right arm under uke's right armpit and extend forwards with your right foot to the rear of uke's posture, exhaling as you do this to help project him across the mat into *ukemi*.

Ryote Dori (*Fig 111*)

The *kokyu nage* projection from this attack comes as uke reaches to grasp both your wrists. Swing your hips back and bring your arms through as you step back with your rearmost foot (left or right depending upon which way you are facing and your balance at the time).

Turn as you extend your arms upwards and over in an undulating motion to project uke past you into forward *ukemi* across the mat.

Irimi Form (*Fig 112*)

As uke steps forwards to grasp both your wrists, step across to uke's side (either right or left depending upon your posture at the time) so that you are facing uke's side with one arm to uke's front and the other to uke's rear. Extend your front arm forwards and down while turning your rear arm to exert forward

Fig 112 (a–b). *Ryote dori kokyu nage, irimi* form.

Fig 112 (b)

Fig 113 (a–b) *Ryote dori kokyu nage*, alternative *irimi* form.

Fig 113 (b)

pressure from behind uke to assist in his forward projection. In this way, uke is eased past you and across the mat into *ukemi*.

Another version of this attack is where uke is led downwards and then up and over to his rear forcing him to make backward *ukemi* (as shown in Fig 113). This can be accomplished with a smooth, flowing motion as the figure indicates, or alternatively as an *atemi* as uke concentrates upon your wrists. This second method is not encouraged for beginners as the possibility of injuries is greatly enhanced.

Ushiro Ryote Dori (Fig 114)

Uke grasps both of your wrists from behind. As he grips your wrists, turn to one side, bringing your centre around so that one of your captured wrists is tucked in front of your centre. Keeping this wrist in front of your centre rotate your arm while extending your hand-blade to your front as you turn your hips

Figs 114(a–d)   *Kokyu nage* from *ushiro ryote dori*.

Fig 114 (b)

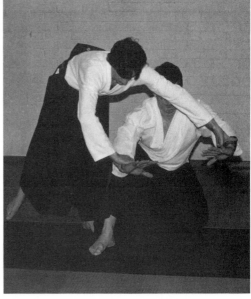

Fig 114 (c)

Fig 114 (d)

back to the other side and slide backwards under uke's arm, unbalancing him forwards. Sink to one knee while extending your arms forwards and downwards to project uke into forward rolling *ukemi*.

Another version of this technique is to scoop both your arms upwards and forwards as you take a step back and to one side. As you bring your arms down in front of you, extend your hands forwards so that uke is forced to perform a forward rolling *ukemi* across the mat.

These are only a few of the techniques available to you as you practise *kokyu nage*. I have chosen to describe these particular ones because they are reasonably simple to put into words; however, many more will be shown to you that are not so easily explained in print. As you progress, you will find certain of these techniques will suit your particular body and style, and which you can perform easily and naturally, while others may not come easily at all.

There are several other techniques that

Figs 115(a–d) *Sumi otoshi*: a variation on *tenchi nage*.

Fig 115 (b)

Figs 116(a–d) Further variation of *sumi otoshi*.

Fig 116 (b)

may be grouped under the heading of *kokyu nage*, but which are actually variations of projection techniques such as *tenchi nage*. A few of these are outlined here.

Sumi Otoshi *(Fig 115)*

As uke reaches forwards to grasp your left wrist with his right hand, move forwards and to your left, extending your left arm downwards and around uke's body to his rear. Dropping your

posture, cut the edge of your right hand into the back of uke's right knee.

The extension of your left hand downwards and towards uke's third point, combined with the cut of your right hand to a vulnerable spot at the back of his knee will force uke backwards to the mat to perform backward *ukemi*. This is a variation on the principle of *tenchi nage* and makes a useful addition to your repertoire.

A further variation occurs as uke steps forwards to grasp your left wrist with his

Fig 115 (c)

Fig 115 (d)

Fig 116 (c)

Fig 116 (d)

Figs 117(a–c) *Aiki otoshi.*   Fig 117 (b)

right hand (*see* Fig 116). Step to your left as you extend your left arm out to your left side and slightly downwards, unbalancing uke to his weak direction. As you enter, make *atemi* to uke's face with your right fist, bringing your hand on to the inside of uke's right elbow. Step forwards with your right foot and continue to extend both arms towards uke's weakest point and slightly downwards.

Lower your body in the direction of your extension and uke will be forced to make *ukemi* across the mat. This variation of *tenchi nage* can be used to good effect when practising *kokyu nage* with several other aikidoka in a group.

Aiki Otoshi (*Fig 117*)

Uke attacks with *migi shomen uchi*, a strike to the top of your head. As he attacks, lower your posture and slide your left leg forwards and to uke's rear, while extending your left arm across the front of uke's abdomen. Uke's strike should now pass across the back of your shoulders.

From this position you may complete the movement in several different ways. The simplest way is to raise your posture and turn to your left into *hidari hanmi*, which will throw uke backwards around to your left side.

Alternatively, you may bring your right hand down to the back of uke's right knee and, as you raise your posture and turn, scoop his right leg up to help you to throw him backwards around your left side.

Kokyu Nage with the *Jo*

The *jo* provides an interesting addition to your *kokyu nage* techniques and it may be used to counter an attack in some situations. The usual practice takes the form of tori offering his *jo* to uke as an invitation to attack and throwing him when he grasps the end of the weapon.

Inherent in all *kokyu nage* technique is the theory of following, and your partners should be well practised in this art as some of the techniques will need careful following in order not to suffer

Fig 117 (c)

Figs 118(a–e)   Basic *jo kokyu nage* – 1.

Figs 118 (b)

Fig 118 (c)

Fig 118 (d)

injuries or lose the technique. Be gentle and careful when wielding your *jo* against other aikidoka, performing flowing movements slowly rather than quick, jerky thrusts. Two simple exercises in the use of the *jo* against an attacker who tries to disarm you are given here. There are many more, but they tend to be quite devastating unless you possess considerable skill.

Exercise 1 (*Fig 118*)

This exercise may be performed to your right or left side, depending on how you are holding the *jo*. It may be performed

to either side of uke, depending on his balance and the relationship between both of your bodies.

Commence in *tsuki no kamae*, offering your *jo* to uke to encourage him to try to take it away from you. As uke takes hold of the *jo*, assuming that you commence in right posture (as in Fig 118), step across to your left with your left foot to draw uke forwards and to his right. Bring your left foot back into right posture as you draw the *jo* back across uke's body and step forwards with your right foot as you raise the *jo* in preparation for the projection.

Lower your posture and direct the tip

Fig 118 (e)

of the *jo* downwards as you gently thrust forwards to project uke across the mat in rolling *ukemi*. Be sure to extend the *jo* towards uke's weakest point and not towards him as this could cause injury.

Exercise 2 (*Fig 119*)

Commence in right posture and offer the *jo* to uke to encourage him to try to take it away from you. As uke grasps the end of your *jo* raise your left hand so that the tip of the *jo* is lowered, drawing uke forwards and to your right side.

Stepping forwards with your left foot, raise the *jo* to extend uke upwards and turn it over uke's head thus making uke turn through 180 degrees. Continue the rotation of the *jo* downwards through the circle and step forwards with your right foot as you extend the *jo* towards uke's weak point. Uke will be projected forwards across the mat.

As I have said before, these are only a couple of the exercises which may be performed in this manner, and further techniques will be taught in your club when you are ready for them. The exercises improve with correct breathing and this must not be ignored just because you are holding a *jo* in your hands. All *kokyu nage* exercises **must** be performed with breath control or they will fail to meet the most important criterion for the exercise.

Relax while performing these techniques and you will soon begin to enjoy them. *Kokyu nage* performed well is not

167

Figs 119(a–e)   Basic *jo kokyu nage* – 2.

Fig 119 (b)

Fig 119 (e)

Fig 119 (c)

Fig 119 (d)

only fun to watch, it is also rewarding to execute and to receive as uke. The more that you enjoy it, the more probable it is that you are becoming better at it. I can only outline some of the techniques; the scope for improvement lies within you.

9 Advanced Techniques

Ueshiba's ideal of 'love for all things' is the ultimate state of awareness for a warrior.

Bob Aubrey (1985)

In this book, I have concentrated on those techniques which are normally expected to be taught to relative beginners. As you progress with your studies, your ability to breakfall will become better and you will gradually become able to accept more advanced technique. This chapter will cover certain techniques in their more advanced forms, which usually involve higher throws and the acceptance of harder breakfalls.

The chapter has been broken down into several sections covering the different areas of aikido and types of technique. This is only a very brief overview of some of the more advanced techniques and is by no means exhaustive. It is intended to give you some insight into the direction in which you will be progressing as you train.

PROJECTION TECHNIQUES

Kote Gaeshi from *Mune Dori* (*Fig 120*)

Partners commence in *ai migi hanmi mune dori*, uke grasping your front lapels with his right hand (*see* Fig 16, page 33). Step back with your right foot

Figs 120(a–d)   *Kote gaeshi* from *mune dori*.

Fig 120 (b)

Fig 120 (c)

Fig 120 (d)

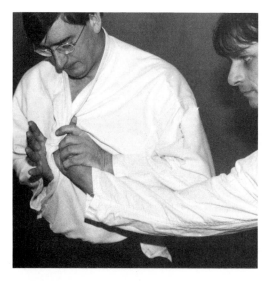

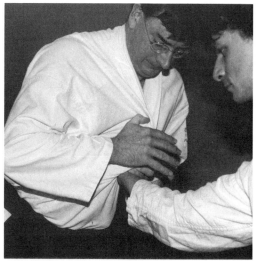

Figs 121(a–b)   Close-up of technique.

Fig 121 (b)

and grasp uke's right wrist with your left hand. Wrap your right hand over uke's, effectively rolling uke's right hand up in the fabric of your *gi* (suit). Roll your upper body backwards, with a semi-circular motion, stepping to the left with your left foot (*see* Fig 121).

Extend your roll around and down to your left, twisting uke's hand over into *kote gaeshi* by using your body and his grip to augment the technique.

Shiho Nage from Yokomen Uchi *(Fig 122)*

Commence in *hidari hanmi* while uke strikes with *yokomen uchi* (*see* Glossary), using his right handblade, to the left side of your head. As the strike commences, step off line to your right into right posture controlling uke's strike with your left hand while you apply *atemi* to his face with your right fist.

Cut uke's right arm down with your left hand to bring his wrist into the palm of your right hand. Continue the motion

through to uke's front third point, turning your right foot to align with this direction. Extend uke's arm out to your front and upwards over your forehead. Step through with your left foot and turn to your right through 180 degress into *migi hanmi*, bringing uke's arm over into *shiho nage*. Cut down to uke's third point to complete the throw.

KOSHI NAGE (HIP THROWS)

These techniques are only practised once you are capable of taking breakfalls from high throws. Uke is taken up over your hip and dropped to the mat on the other side. *Koshi nage* can be performed from most of the recognised forms, the essentials of the technique being that of 'loading up' uke on to your hips with your posture at right-angles to uke's posture, then rotating his body over your lowered hips so that he is thrown over in a high breakfall.

Figs 122(a–d)   *Shiho nage* from *yokomen uchi*.

Fig 122 (b)

Fig 122 (c)

Fig 122 (d)

Figs 123(a–c)   *Koshi nage* from *gyaku hanmi katate dori*.

Fig 123 (b)

Fig 123 (c)

174

Figs 124(a–c)   *Koshi nage* from *yokomen uchi*.

Fig 124 (b)   Fig 124 (c)

Koshi Nage from *Gyaku Hanmi Katate Dori* (*Fig 123*)

Commence with uke holding your left wrist in his right hand. Enter so that your right hip is against uke's centre, bending forwards to push uke's right arm over your head. Lower your body so that you can drape uke across the back of your hips and extend his right arm over your body as you lay uke over your back.

Rotate your hip while transferring your weight across from your right foot to your left foot and continue to extend your left arm outwards and downwards, rotating uke over your hips so that he breakfalls on to the mat beside you.

Koshi Nage from *Yokomen Uchi* (*Fig 124*)

As uke makes *yokomen uchi* strike to the left side of your head, with his right handblade, step forwards and off line into right posture to apply *atemi* to uke's face with your right fist while controlling his right hand with your left. Turn through uke's posture, inserting your right arm under his right shoulder and your left leg and hip into uke's centre. Lower your posture as you lead his right arm over your body and lay uke across the back of your hips.

Straighten your legs and transfer your weight across from your left foot to your right while rotating uke over your hips

Figs 125(a–f) *Ikkyo* from *ushiro ryote dori*.

Fig 125 (b)

to make a high breakfall on to the mat beside you.

USHIRO RYOTE DORI (BOTH WRISTS HELD FROM BEHIND)

In this position, uke is holding both your wrists from behind your back. There are several ways of freeing yourself from such a hold, but the simplest is illustrated in Fig 125, where you turn your body to one side to bring your centre into contact with uke's grip. Keeping your wrist in front of your centre, you may now turn your body round the other way so that you create a space under uke's arm that you can step back through.

Both your wrists will now be in front of you once you have stepped back, and you may apply certain techniques of immobilisation or projection, or you may simply lower your body and extend your wrists as you move backwards, thus propelling uke into forward rolling *ukemi* across the mat.

Ikkyo from *Ushiro Ryote Dori* (*Fig 125*)

From *ushiro ryote dori* turn to your right to bring your centre to your captured right wrist. Keeping the wrist in front of your centre, turn to your left while extending through your right handblade so that you create a space under uke's

Fig 125 (c)

Fig 125 (d)

177

Fig 125 (e)

Fig 125 (f)

right arm into which you may move. Step back under uke's right arm with your right foot while maintaining the extension with your right handblade.

Bring your wrists up in front of you and place your left hand against the back of uke's right elbow to assume control. Turn your right hand up so that you grasp uke's right wrist and extend through his right elbow with your left hand, thumb downwards, to a position in front of your centre. You are now in a position to complete *ikkyo* pinning technique by stepping through uke's posture with your left foot and applying the immobilisation.

DISARMING MOVEMENTS

One of the most important areas of your training is the disarming of your opponent, whatever weapon he is holding. These techniques are usually taught with uke thrusting towards you with a *tanto* (Japanese knife), and you are required to immobilise him while you remove the weapon from his or her grasp.

A dummy wooden knife is commonly used during such training and a great deal of practice is needed before you can graduate to a live blade. Even at high grade, aikidoka have been known to inflict severe wounds upon one another during the practice of various techniques using live blades.

Kote Gaeshi Against a Knife (*Tanken Dori*) (*Fig 126*)

There are several different ways of disarming an opponent armed with a *tanto*, and the following is only one of the recognised techniques. It is offered here

Figs 126(a–g) *Tanken dori*: disarming
movement using *kote gaeshi*.

Fig 126 (b)

Fig 126 (c)

Fig 126 (d)

Fig 126 (e)

Fig 126 (f)

Fig 126 (g)

because it is one of the first to be taught in class, and is both simple and effective.

Uke steps forwards with the *tanto* in his right hand, blade forwards with edge uppermost, to deliver an upward slashing attack to your abdomen. You commence in *migi hanmi* but step across to *hidari hanmi* as you slide your left foot forwards and to your left as the attack commences. Turn with the attack to blend with uke's movement, your left hand dropping naturally over uke's right wrist as the attack is delivered.

Extend uke's knife hand across your centre, delivering *atemi* with your right fist to uke's face. Place your right hand over the back of uke's right hand and turn to your left to perform *kote gaeshi*, throwing uke to the mat. Keep hold of uke's knife hand as you do this. Great care is needed in the early stages of practising this technique to ensure that your right hand does not slip on to the blade.

When uke lands, step around his head, twisting his arm around as you move, which helps to turn uke face down on the mat. You finish in *migi hanmi* with your right foot beside uke's right shoulder. Twist and press downwards on to uke's wrist to apply the *kote gaeshi*; this pressure is sufficient to neutralise uke's grip on the knife. Remove the weapon by pushing it downwards with your right hand, taking the back of the blade between your thumb and forefinger.

Defence Against the *Jo* (*Jo Dori*)

The *jo* is another weapon that you may need to defend yourself against, and there are many different ways of doing this. The following are two simple methods selected to illustrate this defence.

Figs 127(a–c)   Basic *jo dori* 1.

Fig 127 (b)

Fig 127 (c)

181

Figs 128(a–d) Basic *jo dori* 2.

Figs 128 (b)

Fig 128 (c)

Fig 128 (d)

Jo Dori 1 (Fig 127)

Uke thrusts *migi choku tsuki* towards your centre. As he thrusts towards you, step forwards and to your left to allow the thrust to pass across the front of your centre as you assume left posture. Take

hold of the *jo* with both hands, your right hand at the tip of the *jo* and your left hand between uke's hands.

Make a quarter turn to your right, pivoting on your left foot and stepping around with your right foot. Keep the *jo* close to your body as you do this. The *jo*

should now be directed towards uke's rear third point. Step forwards with your left foot and make a gentle but firm thrust forwards and slightly downwards to project uke across the mat away from you.

Jo Dori 2 (Fig 128)

Uke thrusts *hidari choku tsuki* towards your centre. As he thrusts his *jo*, enter with your right foot, moving to your right so that the *jo* passes across in front of your centre. Grasp the *jo* with both hands, your left hand at its tip and your right hand between uke's hands with an overhand grip (as shown in Fig 129).

Raise the *jo* slightly by lowering your left hand and step towards uke's third point with your right foot, gently thrusting forwards and downwards as you consolidate your posture. Uke will be projected forwards across the mat.

HANMI HANDACHI

The term *hanmi handachi* refers to a situation where you are kneeling in *seiza* and uke is attacking from a standing position. This form is often demonstrated in *kokyu nage* exercises, where you move around in *shikko* (knee walking) throwing each attacker as he tries to grab you. Apart from *kokyu nage* exercises, it is possible to perform certain techniques from this position, notably *kote gaeshi*, which lends itself as a defence against such an attack.

Kote Gaeshi from Hanmi Handachi (Fig 130)

Commence by kneeling in *seiza* while uke performs *shomen uchi* strike to the top of your head. To begin with, start the movement from formal *shomen* where your wrists are crossed at fighting

Fig 129 Hand placing for *jo dori* 2.

Figs 130(a–e)   *Kote gaeshi* from *hanmi handachi*.

Fig 130 (b)

Fig 130 (c)

Fig 130 (d)

distance. The following description is given for right-handed application.

As uke comes forward in *migi hanmi*, block his arm with the back of your right wrist. Enter to the left with your left knee, slide your right knee backwards to turn your body to the right and cut uke's arm down so that his right wrist falls into your left hand in front of your centre. Once you have grasped his right wrist in your left hand, transfer your right hand to the back of his right hand in preparation for the performance of the technique.

Slide your left knee back so that you turn your body back to the left as you raise uke's hand in an arc to your left and then downwards, twisting his hand and arm over and outwards. Uke will fall in front of you on to the mat into *ukemi*.

SUWARI WAZA (KNEELING TECHNIQUES)

Hanmi handachi now leads us to consider *suwari waza* (the performance of technique where both uke and tori are in

Fig 130 (e)

a kneeling posture); most techniques may be performed in this fashion. This is derived from the ancient samurai for whom defences were necessary to counter attacks which caught them in *seiza*, a posture they adopted for long periods of time. Samurai were required to spend much time in formal sitting posture, or in *shikko* (walking on their knees). Shikko is practised extensively in aikido where you travel around the mat in a kneeling position. This was the polite way in which the samurai moved around their houses or before dignitaries.

Practice in *shikko* is an essential preliminary to *suwari waza*. Start on your knees with toes turned into the mat under you. Step forwards on to the ball of your left foot, moving forwards over that foot (*see* Fig 131) while pivoting on your right knee. Your right foot should follow closely behind your left foot as you turn a half circle to your right. Move your hips towards your left knee so that it is lowered on to the mat.

To continue, take a step forwards with your right foot, performing the same motions as before but with the opposite

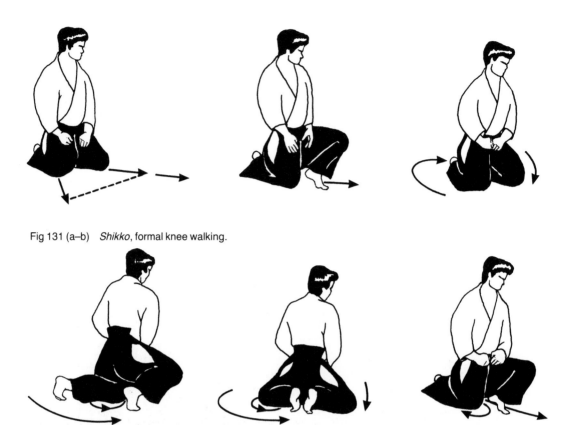

Fig 131 (a–b) *Shikko*, formal knee walking.

Fig 131 (b)

feet, making a half circle to your left. Thus you progress across the mat, turning or travelling straight, depending upon how you perform your *shikko*. It is as well to practise this exercise for at least two or three minutes every day so that you quickly become familiar with it before you are required to execute technique from the posture.

Although techniques may be applied from several forms in *suwari waza*, it is common to commence them from a position of formal *shomen*. Both partners kneel in *seiza* facing one another and uke raises his right (or left) arm to deliver *shomen uchi* strike to the top of your head. You blend by using your right arm

to ensure that the blow will not hit its target.

Ikkyo (Fig 132)

From a position of formal *shomen* push uke's arm upwards and to your right, moving forwards and out to the right with your right knee while applying your left hand, thumb down, to the underside of uke's right elbow. Enter towards uke with your left side, extending your left hand through his elbow and cut downwards with your left hand, guiding uke's arm with your right so that his elbow ends in front of your centre.

Push uke's arm down to the mat with

186

your left hand, easing forwards with your right leg and bringing the knee up behind uke's trapped arm. You are now in a position to apply *ikkyo* immobilisation as described in Chapter 4.

The other immobilisation techniques of *nikkyo*, *sankyo* and *yonkyo* can similarly be applied in *suwari waza* as they all follow a similar pattern.

Irimi Nage (Fig 133)

As in *ikkyo*, commence from a position of formal *shomen*. Make a small entry

with your right knee towards uke's rear, without losing your connection with his extended arm. Then, make a deep step to uke's rear with your left knee. Grasp uke's collar with your left hand at the back and pull his head against your right shoulder. Extend your right arm across the front of uke, leading him upwards and then over backwards, rotating your hips across behind uke as you do this so that he is unbalanced to his rear and rolls backwards on the mat.

Other projection techniques may be practised in *suwari waza*, notably *kote*

Figs 132(a–d) *Ikkyo* from *suwari waza*.

Figs 132 (b)

Fig 132 (c)

Fig 132 (d)

Figs 133(a–d) *Irimi nage* from *suwari waza*.

Fig 133 (b)

188

Figs 133 (c)

Fig 133 (d)

Fig 133 (e)

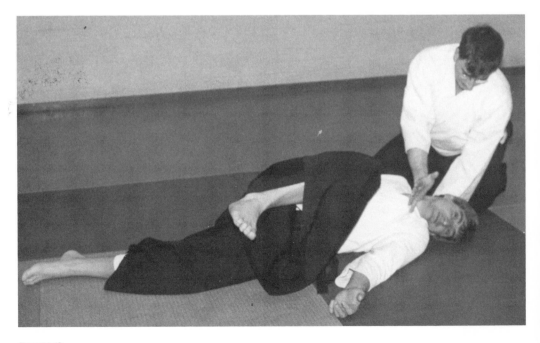

Fig 133 (f)

gaeshi and *tenchi nage*, but *irimi nage* was chosen for this text because of its simplicity.

These are just a few of the techniques you will come across as you progress towards your black-belt grading.

I have made an effort to convey the elements of technique as they are applied in traditional aikido. As you may have noticed by this time, aikido technique can be very elusive and when you have practised one particular technique for many months and are feeling that you really know it well, someone comes along and shows you that yours is only one way to do it and you really know very little about it.

Progress in aikido can be likened to that of a drunken man walking up a hill: he takes four steps forwards and then staggers three steps back, sometimes even more. You must bear in mind that each little step that you take forwards, even if you are knocked back again, will have taught you something. It is through being resilient to all of these setbacks that you will eventually become successful, provided that you measure your success in terms of the values of aikido and not those of contemporary society.

10 Aikido – The Modern Face

*. . . there is not one rigid way of learning and practising but
many ways to achieve the same result. The mountain can be
climbed via several routes. So be humble in your acquisition of
this art and never think yours is the only way.*

Dr Lee Ah Loi (1978)

This book has so far dealt with the teachings of Master Morihei Ueshiba as the basis for learning and perfecting the skills of aikido. His teachings have been split over the years into several different paths. Here the basic techniques of traditional aikido have been emphasised. However, several other schools have evolved which have taken different slants.

The introductory quotation from Dr Lee Ah Loi's book, *Tomiki Aikido*, sums up this concept, although I am led to believe that it is a re-quote from Professor Tomiki. There are obviously several different routes to the same objective, and I shall endeavour to guide you through these so that you will obtain a little understanding of the variety of approaches that exist in the world of aikido.

KI AIKIDO

Founded by Koichi Tohei, this school concentrates upon the development of the individual's *ki* rather than undergoing training across the board (as is presented in this text). The early

teaching is confined to the projection, immobilisation and *kokyu nage* techniques, with practice using *bokken* and *jo* being introduced only at senior levels.

The actual techniques taught in *ki* aikido, however, remain roughly as described within this text, but are performed with the summoning of *ki* as the most important and basic element of their practice.

YOSHIN AIKIDO

This style of aikido was founded by Gozo Shioda, and has a slightly different approach to the art. The instruction stresses positioning and the avoidance of direct lines of attack, while concentrating on basic controls using wrist action and immobilisations. This school has some 150 basic techniques with the emphasis placed upon mental harmony. Competition is not advocated within this system.

Yoshin Aikido has been referred to as a hard style, as Shioda's training methods reflect the gruelling period that he spent as O Sensei's uke. The concept underlying his training is *agatsu*, which may be translated to mean 'control myself'. It is only by blending your mind, strength, energy and ego with that of uke's that you can control both yourself and uke as you wish. In this style, less emphasis is placed upon *ki* than in most others.

TOMIKI AIKIDO

This style was founded by Professor Kenji Tomiki in 1958 at Waseda University (*see* Fig 134). Tomiki was born in 1900, in Akita prefecture, and he commenced training in judo when he was 10 years old. Twelve years later, he entered Waseda University where he met Professor Morihei Ueshiba. He attained 5th Dan Judo in 1928 and eventually was graded to 8th Dan in aikido in 1940, the first of O Sensei's pupils to attain this rank.

After the war, Tomiki travelled to the United States of America to teach judo and aikido, and he returned in 1958 to be appointed as a Professor at Waseda University where he founded the Aikido Club and began to develop his system.

Tomiki felt that in order to encourage young people to take up aikido, the element of competition was required. His philosophy was that once people became interested in the sporting aspects of aikido they would eventually progress to appreciate the deeper spiritual aspect of the art. Tomiki was much influenced by the training methods and philosophies of Dr Jigaro Kano, who was responsible for the evolution of judo from the techniques of ju jutsu. It is interesting to note that judo was Tomiki's first martial art, and the influence of this can be seen to pervade all aspects of his system.

Aikido Kyoghi, as this style is known

Fig 134   Kenji Tomiki.

within Japan, centres around seventeen basic techniques, which are also retained in the form of a *kata*, as was judo in its formative years. The development of Tanto Randori subsequently reflected Tomiki's search for perfection through progress and study. He was endowed with a pool of young students to work with, and this facilitated his development of the more competitive aspects of his system.

Training in Tomiki Aikido does not differ fundamentally from the ways of Traditional Aikido, and the majority of the techniques studied have identical bases in both styles. The Tomiki system

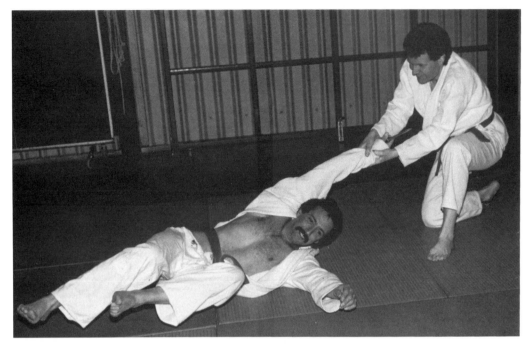

Fig 135(a–c)   Tomiki aikido: *Tanto Randori* contest.

Fig 135 (b)   Fig 135 (c)

Fig 136 1st International Sports-Aikido Open Tournament, 1989. (Courtesy of *Aikido Review*.)

has been in existence for over 25 years and is rapidly spreading outside Japan. In 1970, the first All Japan University Student Aikido Championship was staged, at which time Tanto Randori was introduced into the sport (*see* Fig 135).

The main differences between Tomiki and the Traditional styles is the amount of free play performed by Tomiki students. Free play is usually given more time during sessions than are the formal aspects, and during this time the students will endeavour to reduce their reaction time to attacks and increase their awareness. As in many traditional styles, Tomiki students spend a lot of time working with *tanto, jo* and *bokken* from an early stage in their training. The *bokken* style is centred around the teaching of the Kashima Shinto Ryu, the school where O Sensei studied. It is important

to note that almost all Tomiki students in Britain receive training from Traditional instructors as well as from those specialising in the Tomiki style.

It is difficult to describe the system without delving too deeply into each individual area, and it would require a separate book devoted to the style to do it justice. However, I shall try to provide a very brief outline of the elements of Tomiki training and an overview of the techniques.

Basic Techniques

The basis of the system is *tai sabaki* (body movement) to teach avoidance of attacks, and *sen-no-sen* (attack within attack), an important element for the effectiveness of technique. This latter element has not been dealt with in this text but both are taught within traditional

195

Fig 137   Tomiki aikido: *Ninin Dori* contest.

styles. In simple terms, tori acts at the moment the attacker launches his attack, so shortening the distance between himself and uke while gaining the initiative and control over the attacker before his attack is completed.

The basic wrist techniques taught during training are all essentially similar to those in this book, with one or two exceptions, and some of the names of the techniques are different.

Randori No kata

The techniques in the *randori no kata* form the basis for the Tomiki system upon which the various forms of competition are built. The *kata* should be performed at a realistic attack speed and is practised from an attack distance of six feet. There are seventeen basic movements commencing with defensive blocks, strikes and blending movements, progressing through immobilisation techniques and armlocks to projection techniques and finishing in the style of *kokyu nage*.

Ura Waza

At the same time that you are learning the techniques of the *randori no kata*, counters to each of the techniques are also being taught. This provides students with the basis upon which to compete with one another.

196

Competition

There were originally four types of competition practised within the system, each having its own separate rules according to its purpose and to the style practised. The rules differ from area to area so they cannot be outlined definitively. Suffice it to say that, generally, the rules follow the broad lines upon which judo competition is based. Considering that Professor Tomiki was schooled in judo competition for many years before he commenced his study of aikido, this is hardly surprising. The types of contest are as follows.

Kata Competition

Contestants choose the *kata* they wish to demonstrate. This is similar to judo *kata* in that each *kata* is performed by two students who must demonstrate strict control, synchronisation and co-ordination of their movements in both kneeling and standing positions. A scoring system is used which follows the same lines as that for gymnastics where five judges award points for each contestant.

Ninin Dori

This is freestyle competition with three contestants on the mat at the same time. Two act as attackers and one is defending. The defender is judged upon the variation of his defence techniques, speed of performance and his control under conditions of stress as he is being attacked by both opponents. The competition lasts for three minutes, each contestant acting as tori for one minute. The defender is required to

Fig 138   Tanto Randori at the Mike Hynes 'All England' Open Championship 1989. (Courtesy of *Aikido Review*.)

manoeuvre his attackers in such a way that they can only attack one at a time, unless he is in a position to use their simultaneous attack to his advantage.

Randori Kyoghi

This is no longer a form of competition within the Tomiki style, but is now a system of light training where two unarmed students compete against one another. These sessions follow similar lines to *randori* sessions practised in sports-style judo.

Tanto Randori

This is the most commonly practised form of aikido contest in Japan. In order to perform it successfully, it is necessary to know the techniques of the *tanto randori no kata*, which are based on the techniques of the *randori no kata*. (Fig 138).

Two players, one armed with a dummy knife or soft batten, compete against one another. The player with the knife is the attacker and the unarmed defender scores by demonstrating his skill in avoidance of the attacks, and by his application of good aikido techniques. The attacker can also score by making strikes to the target area on his opponent. The designated target area is any part of the trunk between armpits and waistline. Limbs and face are not to be attacked.

Tomiki aikido, although competitive by nature, has not permitted the sports side to dominate the practice of technique as has judo in recent years. It is not aimed just at the young students who wish to compete, but it is there for all people to enjoy. Thus there are two ways of practising within the art: the traditional way

through study of *kata*, and the sports way through competition with one another.

Generally, there is one syllabus for seniors and another for juniors up to and including sixteen years old. The junior syllabus may contain a varied number of stages according to the individual or regional governing body. Locking and twisting techniques are not permitted to be performed upon juniors as these could damage their bone structure. For the juniors, the emphasis is on good posture and movement.

In the senior syllabus in Britain, all students grade through the study of the theoretical side of aikido, although they must have a good understanding of the rules of competition. Success in competition does not count towards gradings, and there is no penalty for not taking part in contests. The majority of Tomiki students in Britain do not take part in any form of competition.

Following on from the basic instruction in *randori no kata*, the student progresses on to the six formal *koryu no Kata*, which make up the complete system.

Koryu Dai Ichi

Twenty-four techniques commencing in *suwari waza* (kneeling) and proceeding on to *tachi waza* (standing techniques). This forms the basis of all the other *Koryu no kata*) in the series.

Koryu Dai Ni

Sixteen techniques all performed in *tachi waza*. The first eleven techniques are demonstrated from a position where uke is grasping tori's wrist or wrists, while the final five techniques are defences against handblade attacks to tori's temple.

Koryu Dai San

This *kata* introduces the use of the sword and *jo*. Techniques are performed in defence against unarmed attacks, and then attackers armed with knife, *bokken* and *jo*. Later sections include *tori* defending by the use of both *jo* and *bokken*. A total of fifty techniques are demonstrated during this *kata*.

Koryu Dai Yon

A *kata* based on techniques of breaking the balance of uke, including some

Fig 139 *Tanto dori – shomen giri gedan ate.*

Fig 140 *Tanto dori – kote goeshi.*

standing techniques and counters totalling twenty-five movements in all.

Koryu Dai Go

Twenty-three techniques, seven of which are performed in *suwari waza*. The *kata* is demonstrated with speed but not at the expense of accuracy of technique.

Koryu Dai Roku

Demonstrated slowly and with grace, these thirty-nine techniques include *suwari waza*, *tachi waza* and defences against *tanto* and *bokken* as well as techniques where tori utilises both *bokken* and *jo*.

As you will have gathered there is a considerable depth of knowledge required within the Tomiki system, and there are many similarities between Tomiki and Traditional aikido. Tomiki aikido has borrowed some of its style from the teachings of Dr Jigaro Kano and his Kodokan Judo system. The concept of learning by the demonstration of *kata* was the original method of training for judo as well as for karate and many other of the martial arts and, as such, Tomiki aikido has followed the more formalised path taken by the sports side of the martial arts (Fig 143).

It is understood that when Tomiki first developed his sports style, he offered it to O Sensei who initially accepted it. His

Fig 141   *Suwari waza – tenka kote hineri.*

Fig 142 *Suwari waza – kote gaeshi* immobilisation.

Fig 143   Detailed instruction being given during the *Kikusui Kai*, Sutton Martial Arts Centre, Seminar, December 1989. (Courtesy of *Aikido Review*.)

committee of senior students, however, rejected Tomiki's ideas, so O Sensei suggested to Tomiki that he should continue in his development of the sports side under the title of Tomiki Aikido. For this reason, Ueshiba still retains the great respect of all Tomiki aikidoka.

There are many other styles and schools of aikido apart from those that I have devoted space to in this chapter, and these include the following list, which is by no means complete:

***Korindo* aikido** Founded by ̄Minoru Hirai, a self-defence system.
Shinwa taido Founded by Yoichiro Inoue, a self-defence and sports system.
***Otsuki ryu* aikido** Founded by Yutaka Otsuki, a self-defence system.

Kobu jutsu Founded by Tetsuomi Hoshi, a self-defence system.
Shin riaku heiho Founded by Setaro Tanaka, a self-defence and combat system.
Yae ryu Founded by Harunosuke Fukui; no further details available.
Shindo rokugo ryu Founded by Senryuken Noguchi, a self-defence system.

All of the above schools of aikido, and several others, are essentially similar in technique basis, their difference being purely the areas in aikido that are stressed by their masters. Tomiki aikido and Traditional Iwama style could be shown as being opposite poles of an aikido continuum, with the other styles and schools fitting somewhere in between them.

Although the underlying philosophies of all the styles remain the same, it is the way in which the training is applied that differs. Some styles will lean towards the development of *ki* while others advocate the concept of harmony between uke and tori. The weapons such as the sword and the jo are seen as fundamental to many traditional styles, while other schools tend to relate their techniques to *tai jutsu* (body technique) rather than to weapons.

The concept of competition in aikido was pioneered by Professor Kenji Tomiki and this has appealed to many students who are looking for a more sporting side to their lives. In modern times, the competitive spirit has tended to outweigh the fulfilment provided by perfection of technique, and a martial art that offers no form of competition is sometimes looked upon by many as being worthless. There are arguments for and against competition within the martial arts, and I do not intend to discuss these at this time. It was Tomiki's idea that some of those who are attracted to aikido purely by the sporting aspects will eventually proceed beyond competition to embrace the deeper aspects of the martial art, and this has indeed been proven to be the case in latter years.

It is untrue to say that students who take up traditional styles of aikido are those to whom contest means little, and many traditional students are known to enter open aikido competitions, although mainly those involving *kata*. The percentage of aikido students who enter competition from any of the associations and styles remains virtually consistent at 4.5 per cent, a figure which exactly reflects the national figure for athletes entering competitions. There is little doubt that there is a demand for contest, and Tomiki style offers this element, although the choice whether or not to take part is still up to the individual without influence in either direction by his instructors.

There are many bodies in Britain that have been set up to promote aikido in its various forms and I have listed some of these in Appendix 3, with as much detail of their organisations as I can obtain. Readers may wish to contact them to establish the location of suitable clubs in their areas.

Glossary of Terms

Ai   Harmony or unification.
Ai hanmi   Mutual stance where both partners have the same foot advanced.
Aiki   Blending or harmonising of *ki*.
Aikido   The way of harmony of the spirit.
Aikidogi   Suit worn by persons practising aikido. This may be a lightweight karate or judo suit.
Aikidoka   Person who practises aikido.
Aiki ken   Aiki sword techniques.
Atemi   A defensive strike used to neutralise the *ki* of your opponent. In aikido, this is not meant to inflict injury.
Awase   To combine. The term used in aikido to denote techniques executed by both partners which mutually combine, such as *ken* or *jo* combinations.

Barai *see* Harai
Bo   Straight pole about six feet long.
Bokken   Curved wooden practice sword.
Bu   Martial ardour or spirit.
Budo   Martial ways.
Budoka   One who practises the martial ways.
Bushido   Way of the warrior. The strict code of ethical behaviour followed by the Samurai warriors.

Choku tsuki   Straight thrust, usually with the *jo*, to your partner's centre.

Dan   Rank or degree. The term used for anyone who has achieved at least first degree black belt.
Deshi   Disciple or trainee.

Do   The way, truth or path whereby one may harmonise body and mind.
Dojo   Training hall where the way is practised.
Doshu   Grandmaster. A hereditary position, Kisshomaru Ueshiba currently being the *Aikido Doshu*.

Empi   Elbow.
Eri   Collar or lapel that runs round the front of the *aikidogi*.

Fuchi   The metal sleeve at the base of the handle of a *katana*, next to the guard.
Fudo no shisei   Immovable posture, either sitting or standing.

Gaeshi (kaeshi)   Outward turning movement or counter.
Gedan   Lower area of the body.
Gedan gaeshi   Circular *jo* movement aimed at the lower part of opponent's body.
Gedan tsuki   *Jo* thrust aimed at the lower part of opponent's body.
Gi   Uniform or suit.
Gokyo   Fifth pinning technique.
Goshi (koshi)   Hip.
Gyaku   Opposite or alternate.
Gyaku hanmi   Stance where partners have opposite feet advanced.

Habaki   Collar around the blade of the *katana*. It ensures a tight fit between scabbard and blade.
Hachi no ji   *Jo* movement based on the Japanese character for eight.

Hakama Traditional skirt-like trousers worn by *aikidoka* and other high-ranking martial artists.

Hanmi Stance or posture.

Hanmi handachi Situation where one person is sitting and the other is standing.

Happo giri Eight direction cut – a sword exercise.

Hara Centre.

Harai (barai) Sweep. The sweeping of an opponent's *ken* or *jo* away and down-wards.

Hasso no kamae Posture with *ken* or *jo* vertical at the right shoulder.

Hasso gaeshi Moving from basic posture to *hasso no kamae*.

Henke Blending.

Hidari Left.

Hito e mi Making the posture small.

Ho Direction.

Hombu Headquarters.

I dori Seated defence.

Iai Swordplay. Sword exercises using a series of cutting and thrusting techniques while drawing and returning the blade.

Iaido The modern art of drawing the sword from its scabbard.

Ikkyo First pinning technique.

Irimi Entering movement.

Irimi nage Entering throw.

Irimi tenkan Combined entering and turning movement.

Iro obi Coloured belt.

Jo Straight pole about four feet long.

Jo dori Techniques for disarming an opponent armed with a *jo*.

Jodan Upper areas of opponent's body.

Jodan gaeshi Circular *jo* strike to upper part of your opponent's body.

Joseki Place where honoured guest is seated in the dojo.

Juji nage Crossed arms throw.

Kaiten Open and turn.

Kaiten nage Spiral throw.

Kamae The combative stance assumed when facing an opponent.

Kansha Gratitude.

Kata Predetermined sequences in set forms. Also means shoulder.

Kata dori Uke holds tori's upper arm at the shoulder.

Katana Long curved sword used by the Samurai warriors.

Katate dori Uke holds tori's wrist in one hand.

Ken Sword.

Ken no kamae Posture when holding sword or bokken in readiness for action.

Kenjutsu Aikido techniques performed while holding the sword.

Ki The vital force or energy of the body.

Ki musubi Uniting your *ki* with that of your opponent.

Kiai An explosive outpouring of vital energy, manifested as a piercing shout from the depths of one's being.

Kogeki Attack.

Kokyu Breath power.

Kokyu dosa Exercise of extending *ki*.

Kokyu ho Breath meditation. Used as an exercise in *kokyu dosa* from a standing position.

Kokyu nage Throwing with breath power.

Kokyu undo Breath movement. Techniques used to develop breath power performed from sitting or standing postures, individually or with a partner.

Koshi nage Hip throw.

Kote Wrist.

Kote gaeshi Throw by application on the wrist of a turn-out movement.

Kumi jo Partner exercises with the *jo*.

Kumi tachi Partner exercises with the sword.

Ma-ai Fighting distance.
Mae Front or forward.
Men Head.
Migi Right.
Morote dori One wrist held by two hands.
Mune Chest.
Mune dori One hand gripping the *gi* at the centre of the chest.
Mune tsuki Thrusting attack to the centre of the chest.

Nagare Flowing.
Nagare gaeshi Strike front and rear in a flowing movement.
Nage Throw.
Nikkyo The second pinning technique.

O Sensei Common way of referring to Sensei Ueshiba, the founder of aikido.
Oi Centre, abdomen.
Oi tsuki Thrust to the centre.
Omote Moving forwards.
Orenai te Unbendable arm.

Rei The bow, a formal gesture of respect and gratitude.
Renzoku Continuous.
Ryote dori Both wrists being held by your partner.

Sabaki Movement.
Sankyo The third pinning movement.
Seika no tanden One point (centre).
Seiza The formal sitting position.
Sensei The formal title used for the teacher.
Shihan Master instructor.
Shiho nage Four-direction throw.
Shiho giri Four-direction cut with the sword.
Shikko Knee walking.
Shimoza Lower seat of the dojo; The side where students sit between practices.

Shomen Centre of the head. Also the high side of the *dojo*.
Shomen uchi Strike straight down to the centre of the head.
Sode Sleeve.
Sode dori Attack holding the sleeve just above the elbow.
Suburi Solo practice of individual *jo* or *bokken* movements.
Suwari Kneeling.
Suwari waza Techniques performed in a kneeling posture.

Tacherei Standing bow.
Tachi Sword.
Tachi dori Techniques used to disarm an opponent who has a sword.
Tai Body.
Tai jutsu Body techniques performed without weapons.
Tai no henko Basic blending practice.
Tai sabaki Body movement.
Tanren uchi *Bokken* practice for developing the centre.
Tanto Knife.
Tatami The mat upon which you practise aikido.
Tegatana Handblade technique where the hand, with fingers spread to project *ki*, functions as a sword.
Tenchi Heaven and earth.
Tenchi nage Heaven and earth throw.
Tenkai Stepping move with turn.
Tenkan Turning move with step.
Toma At a great distance.
Tori Person who performs the throwing technique.
Tsuki Thrust.
Tsuki no kamae Posture holding the jo in readiness to thrust.

Uchi Strike. Also means 'inside'.
Uchi deshi Inner disciple, who lives at the dojo acting as a twenty-four-hour trainee/attendant to the Master.

Uchi komi   Stepping forwards and striking.

Uchi mawari   To step inside your partner's arm.

Uchi tachi   One of a pair practising *kumi tachi* (the attacking partner).

Uke   Person who performs *ukemi*.

Ukemi   Breakfall.

Uke tachi   One of a pair practising *kumi tachi* (the defending partner).

Ura   Back (uke's)

Ura sankaku   Back triangular stance.

Ushiro   Back (tori's).

Ushiro waza   Techniques applied when you are attacked from the rear.

Waza   Technique.

Yoko   Side.

Yokomen   Side of head.

Yokomen uchi   Strike to the side of opponent's head.

Yonkyo   The fourth pinning technique.

Zanshin   Unbroken spirit. The concentrated connection that remains with your partner even after the technique has been completed.

Zarei   Kneeling bow.

Zengo   Forward and backward.

Zori   Slip-on sandal made of straw.

Appendix 1

JAPANESE FOR AIKIDOKA

Aikido is an art which has sprung from the old Japanese fighting ways and, as such, it is steeped in tradition. It is for this reason that the art recognises and continues many of the traditional ways of *budo* which have tended to fall by the wayside in other martial arts. Much of the etiquette has been covered in earlier chapters; however, it is also essential for all students to become familiar with the use of Japanese terminology.

Japanese names for techniques and the language of the dojo is nowadays sadly lacking in many martial arts and is often given no more than perfunctory consideration. In Traditional Aikido, the cultural aspects have been retained as much as possible, and the Japanese language is now studied at basic level. In some clubs, a knowledge of basic Japanese is essential for certain grading examinations. That is not to say that aikidoka must be

a. Peter   *Pi – te – ru*

b. Brian   *Bu – ra – i – a – n*

c. John   *Jo – n*

d. Mark   *Ma – ku*

e. Angela   *A – n – ge – ra*

Fig 144   Examples of names converted to *Katakana* script.

able to converse in Japanese, but they must understand what is being asked and must be able to translate the commands and possess a knowledge of the language of the dojo, as well as that of the country of origin.

The Language

There are about 120 million people living in Japan, and their language is now being studied by an increasing number of businessmen, although Japanese is by no means international. The Japanese language is relatively easy to speak and understand, and many English words are commonly used in the modern language.

The Japanese adopted the Chinese system of writing to fit their own language over a thousand years ago and there are three writing systems in use. *Kanji*, or Sino-Japanese characters, is the commonly used script for the words of the language, while *katakana* is used primarily to write foreign words and names. *Hiragana* is used for verb conjugations and as syntax markers.

The pronunciation of Japanese must

bya	cha	gya	hya	kya	mya
ビャ	チャ	ギャ	ヒャ	キャ	ミャ
byo	cho	gyo	hyo	kyo	myo
ビョ	チョ	ギョ	ヒョ	キョ	ミョ
byu	chu	gyu	hyu	kyu	myu
ビュ	チュ	ギュ	ヒュ	キュ	ミュ
nya	pha	rya	sha		
ニャ	ビャ	リャ	シャ		
nyo	pho	ryo	sho		
ニョ	ビョ	リョ	ショ		
nyu	phu	ryu	shu		
ニュ	ビュ	リュ	シュ		

Fig 145 *Katakana* with romanised pronunciation.

Fig 146 *Katakana* with romanised pronunciation.

first be studied, although most of the sounds are similar to those found in English. Japanese is usually broken up into syllables, each containing a consonant and a vowel, for example, AI-KI-DO. There is no stress on any one syllable – equal weight should be given to all syllables of each word. The most common system of writing Japanese in English is the Hepburn system of romanisation, and this is the one that English speakers usually find simplest.

Vowels

a Pronounced rather flat and staccato as in 'cart', but a little more clipped.
e Pronounced as in 'pet'.
i Pronounced like the 'ea' in 'heat', but more clipped.
o Pronounced as in 'lot', but with lips more rounded.
u Pronounced as in 'Sue'. At the end of words, it is often silent, for example, 'desu' is pronounced 'dess'.

Long vowels Where a vowel is printed with a line above it, as in ā, it is pronounced double its usual length. The long vowel 'i' is usually written 'ii'.

Where two vowels appear together they are pronounced as indicated above, thus the Japanese word 'tai' would be pronounced as the English word 'tie' and not 'tay'.

Consonants

Most consonants are pronounced similarly to English, with the following exceptions:

g Always pronounced hard as in 'give' rather than softly as in 'gin'.
f Pronounced to give a sound midway between the English 'f' and 'h'.
r Pronounced almost like 'l', quickly and lightly but not rolled.

Long consonants Similar to the long vowel, these are pronounced individually. For example the **nn** in *Konnichi wa* is like 'one night' and not as in 'Sunny', and the **pp** in Nippon is like 'skip past' and not as in 'nipper'.

Everyday Expressions

Greetings

Hello	*Konnichi wa* (used from late morning onwards)
Goodbye	*Sayōnara* (familiar); *Shitsurei shimasu* (polite/formal)
Good morning	*Ohayō Gozaimasu*
Good evening	*Konban wa*
Good night	*Uyasumi* (familiar); *Oyasumi nasai (polite)*

General

Thank you	*Dōmo*
	Arigatō

Thank you very much	*Dōmo arigatō*
	Dōmo arigatō gozaimasu (for something happening now)
	Dōmo arigatō gozaimashita (for something which has just happened or ended)
You're welcome	*Dō itashimashite*
Please	*Dōzo* (do, or go ahead).
Excuse me	*Sumamasen*
Welcome	*Irasshaimase*
Yes	*Hai*
No	*Iie*
Good	*Ii*
Bad	*Warui*
No good	*Dame*

Writing in Japanese

It has become popular to wear a belt with your name embroidered down one side and the organisation (judo, karate and so on) down the other. There are some firms that provide a service by which they hold a stock of belts with the main recognised organisations embroidered on one side. You are usually required to supply the Japanese characters which spell your name for the stitching on the other side.

The tables which follow show the *katakana* syllables with the romanised pronunciations over them. To make up your name, you need to break it down into its component syllables and make as near a phonetic match as possible. Certain sounds are not reproduced too well in Japanese, such as the 'll' in Will, and this should be converted to 'Wiru'. Names ending in 's', such as Des, should be transformed to 'Desu' for the purpose of conversion into *katakana*.

Examples of some names are given in Fig 144 to show how the translations should take place.

Appendix 2

TYPICAL GRADING SYLLABUS

Aikido, by nature a dynamic martial art, is constantly in a state of change. The methods of performing the techniques are continually being improved upon by the masters, and such revisions take some time to filter down to club level in the Western hemisphere. It is quite possible that some of the techniques outlined in this text will have been subject to revision by the time you read this, although the Iwama style upon which this book is based endeavours to keep to the methods as taught by O Sensei up until his death. Thus the Iwama style will probably be subject to less change than many of the other styles.

Accepting that aikido is in a permanent state of flux (to one degree or another), it follows that the criteria laid down for the grading of students will also be subject to variation. There is not a formalised syllabus set out by a governing body which details the requirements for the gradings that you will take, and it appears that each club or complex of clubs formulates its own syllabus. Thus it would be impossible to state with certainty which techniques should be studied for any particular grading, and only very general guidelines can be offered.

To give an indication of the levels of technique required for each grade I have included a typical grading syllabus which is currently in use at the club where I train. Two things should be borne in mind when studying this syllabus. Firstly, it is subject to revision from time to time and has been changed at least twice, to my knowledge. Secondly, the introduction of weapon techniques and the importance placed upon them will depend upon the particular instructor and his view of aikido, his preferences and the style practised.

Grading for 5th Kyu (Yellow Belt)

As this is the first grading that you will take, the emphasis is placed upon the basics. On average, it should take about six months of training to reach the required standard.

Basics

Tai no henko
Kokyu ho
Kokyu dosa

Techniques	Pinning techniques: *ikkyo, nikkyo* and *sanyo*. Projection techniques: *shiho nage, irimi nage, kote gaeshi* and *tenchi nage*. All techniques to be performed from *ai hanmi katate dori* and *gyaku hanmi katate dori* (1st and 2nd forms) to right and left sides.
Weapons	*Bokken* (first three *ken suburi*).

Grading for 4th Kyu (Orange Belt)

After a further six months' training, the next grading incorporates the previous syllabus, plus the following:

Basics	*Tai no henko* from *ki no nagare*. *Kokyu dosa* – three variations (side, over and under holds).
Techniques	*Sode dori* (3rd form) techniques to left and right sides, demonstrating the same techniques as listed for the previous grading.
Kokyu nage	Five techniques to be demonstrated to *ai hanmi katate dori* and *gyaku hanmi katate dori*.
Weapons	*Bokken* – all seven *ken suburi*. *Jo* – first five *jo suburi*.

Grading for 3rd Kyu (Green Belt)

The time taken for training for this grading will depend on the amount of sessions that you undertake and how quickly you can assimilate the knowledge. This grading incorporates all the techniques for the two previous gradings, plus the following:

Basics	*Tai no henko* from *ki no nagare*, special emphasis being placed upon posture and balance. *Kokyu dosa* – five variations (side, over and under, plus firm pin and upper-arm hold).
Techniques	*Mune dori* (4th form) techniques to all the previous pinning and projection techniques except *shiho nage*.
Kokyu nage	Continuous techniques in *ai hanmi katate dori* and *gyaku hanmi katate dori* with two or three ukes.
Shomen uchi	Any four techniques as requested.
Suwari waza	*Shomen uchi* – *ikkyo*, *irimi nage* and *kote gaeshi*.
Weapons	*Bokken* – *Aiki ken no awase* to *migi* and *hidari*. First *kumi tachi*. *Jo* – all twenty *jo suburi* and first two *kumi jo*. First twelve moves of *Aiki jo no sanjuichi no kata* (31-count *jo kata*).

Grading for 2nd Kyu (Blue Belt)

This grading incorporates all the requirements for the previous gradings plus the following:

Techniques	Any techniques from *ai hanmi katate dori* through to *yokomen uchi* (1st – 6th forms).
Kokyu nage	*Kokyu nage* from any holding attack with two or three ukes.
Weapons	*Bokken* – all four *aiki ken no awase*. All *kumi tachi*. *Jo* – *aiki jo no sanjuichi no kata*. First twelve moves of the *aiki jo no sanjuichi no kata no kumijo*. First five *kumi jo*.
Language	An understanding of basic Japanese is required.

Grading for 1st Kyu (Brown Belt)

This grading incorporates all the requirements for the previous gradings plus the following:

Techniques

Any techniques from *ai hanmi katate dori* through to *oi tsuki* (1st − 7th forms). *Gyaku hanmi shiho nage* − explanation of the four directions.

Kokyu nage

Kokyu nage from striking attacks controlling uke's position in order to block other attackers.

Weapons

Bokken − all *awase* techniques demonstrating good blending and maintaining *zanshin. Ki musubi no tachi. Tachi dori.*
Jo − full *aiki jo no sanjuichi no kata no kumijo* (31-move *kata* with partner). *Tanto* − *tanken dori* (disarming).

Counters

Basic counters to incorrectly performed techniques.

Appendix 3

ORGANISATIONS REPRESENTING AIKIDO IN BRITAIN

The only aikido body officially recognised in the United Kingdom by both the Martial Arts Commission and the Sports Council is the British Aikido Board, which comprises the following sixteen organisations:

Aikido Development Society
Aikido Fellowship
Aikido Research Foundation
Aikido Society of Wales
British Aikido Association
British Yoshinkan Federation
Ellis School of Traditional Aikido
Institute of Aikido
Kai Shin Kai
Kolesnikov's School of Mind and Body
   Development
Lancashire Aikikai
National Aikido Federation
Shudokan Institute of Aikido
United Kingdom Aikikai
United Kingdom Aikido Federation
Washi Aikido Federation

The British Aikido Board was set up in conjunction with the MAC and Sports Council in order that properly constituted organisations could attach themselves to an umbrella body providing the general public with access to bona fide aikido clubs. The British Aikido Board developed into the official governing body whose objectives include increasing public awareness of aikido, making available to the public a source of information regarding the whereabouts of clubs in specific areas and ensuring that organisations follow set codes of practice under suitable coaches.

The British Aikido Board
Contact: David Timms
6 Halkingcroft
Langley
Slough
Berks SL3 7AT

There are several other organisations which represent aikido in Britain and these, although not members of the BAB, appear to have ideals that are just as high. The following is a list of organisations, including some BAB members:

The Amateur Aikido Association
Contact: Chris Moslin
48 Trenchard Crescent
Nabbotts Farm Estate
North Springfield
Chelmsford
Essex CH1 5FG

This association has national and international recognition and caters for all styles of aikido. There are no association fees payable and the objective of the association is to allow members to practise any style of aikido.

The British Aikido Association
Contact: Vince Sumpter
65 Vanner Road
Witney
Oxon OX8 6LL

This association caters for both competitive and traditional styles of aikido. It was founded in 1968 in order to promote and maintain the ethical and technical standards of aikido. It has established a coaching and promotion structure which is recognised by the All Japan Aikido Association.

This association incorporates the *Kai Shin Kai* and is a member of the BAB. It is reputed to be the biggest aikido organisation in Britain.

The British Aikido Council
Contact: Paul Wildish
33 High House Avenue
Wymondham
Norfolk

This is a young organisation formed to preserve the character of the Tomiki school in Britain and to promote training and technical interchange with the Hombu dojos of the All Japan Aikido Association. Maintaining and extending these links, by holding summer camps and seminars led by senior instructors from Japan, is seen as vital to the technical development of Koygi aikido in Britain.

The British Aikido Federation
Contact: Peter Megann
Yew Tree Cottage
Toot Baldon
Oxon OX9 9NE

The British Aikido Federation and its student wing, the BUAF, comprises about 60 clubs from all over England and Wales. It is recognised by the Aikido World Headquarters and members of the International Aikido Federation and the European Aikido Federation.

The BAF teaching syllabus is closely based upon that of the Hombu dojo in Tokyo. Competition is excluded within its clubs.

The English Aikido Union
Contact: Mrs C. Wolfendale
83 Ravensworth
Ryhope
Sunderland
Tyne and Wear SR2 0BH

No details have been received about this organisation.

The Institute of Aikido
Contact: David Timms
6 Halkingcroft
Langley
Slough
Berks SL3 7AT

This organisation was reconstituted following the demise of the Renown Aikido Society, which went back as far as 1957. A founder member of the BAB, the Institute caters for many clubs throughout Great Britain, and maintains the highest standards within its ranks.

UK Aikikai
Contact: Anne Milner
Milestone Cottage
Old Alcester Road
Portway
Nr Birmingham B48 7NT

This organisation caters only for traditional-style aikido as taught by O Sensei and continued by his son, Kissho-maru. It is affiliated to the Hombu dojo in Tokyo, and its Technical Director is Chiba Sensei, who visits the UK annually in order to help maintain the technical standards.

The organisation's chief instructor is M. Smith (5th Dan) and there are some 45 clubs affiliated throughout the United Kingdom.

Bibliography

The following books are referred to in the text and quotations have been included from the majority of them. Most of these volumes are still in print or can be obtained from public libraries.

Aubry, Bob, *Aikido and the New Warrior* (R. Heckler Ed.), (North Atlantic Books, 1985)

Corcoran, John and Farkas, Emil, *Martial Arts: Traditions, History, People* (Gallery Books, 1988)

Farkas, Emil and Corcoran, John, *The Overlook Martial Arts Dictionary* (The Overlook Press, 1983)

Klickstein, Bruce, *Living Aikido* (North Atlantic Books, 1987)

Loi, Dr Lee Ah, *Tomiki Aikido (Vols 1 & 2)* (Paul H. Crompton Ltd, 1978/79)

Random, Michel, *The Martial Arts* (Peerage Books, 1987)

Saito, Morihiro, *Traditional Aikido, Vol 1* (Minato Research & Publishing Co. Ltd, 1973)

Saito, Morihiro, *Aikido, Its Heart and Appearance* (Minato Research & Publishing Co. Ltd, 1975)

Shioda, Gozo, *Dynamic Aikido* (Kodansha International Ltd, 1968)

Stevens, John, *Aikido, The Way of Harmony* (Shambhala Publications, 1984)

Ueshiba, Kisshomaru, *Aikido* (Hozansha Publishing, 1974)

Ueshiba, Kisshomaru, 'Interview with Doshu' (from *Aiki News*, 1978)

Westbrook, Adele and Ratti, Oscar, *Aikido and the Dynamic Sphere* (Chas E. Tuttle Co., 1979)

Williams, Bryn (Ed.), *Martial Arts of the Orient* (Galley Press, 1987)

Index

222